Le Mot Juste

Le Mot Juste

A Dictionary of Classical & Foreign Words & Phrases

Editorial panel: John Buchanan-Brown,
Jennifer Cang, John Crawley, Barbara Galushka, Brendan McCabe,
Gilman Parsons, Carol Steiger, Kate Williams

VINTAGE BOOKS

A DIVISION OF RANDOM HOUSE

NEW YORK

First Vintage Books Edition, February 1981
Copyright © 1980, 1981 by Kogan Page
All rights reserved under International and Pan-American
Copyright Conventions. Published in the United States by
Random House, Inc., New York. Originally published by Kogan
Page Limited, London, in 1980 and reprinted in 1981

Library of Congress Cataloging in Publication Data
Main entry under title:
Le Mot juste: a dictionary of classical & foreign
words & phrases.
Reprint of the ed. published by Kogan Press, London.
1. English language—Foreign words and phrases—
Dictionaries. I. Buchanan-Brown, John.
PE1670.M67 1981   422′.4′03   80-6122
ISBN 0-394-74690-2

Manufactured in the United States of America

Contents

General Introduction

When Sam Goldwyn, from the deck of his liner, called out *bon voyage* to his friends on the receding shore, he got it nearly right, but not quite. This book is intended to help not only the Sam Goldwyns among us, but all those who do not know the meaning or correct use of a term from a foreign language which is commonly used in English, but not always understood, even by 'sophisticated' people. Often they are specialized legal terms. Lawyers know *ignoratio legis non exculpat* (ignorance of the law is no excuse), but the rest of us may be excused for not having it at our fingertips. Musicians know the meaning of *allegro ma non troppo* (briskly but not too much so), but many of the audience may have to guess. Not only specialists, but some communities, such as English-speaking Jews, have introduced terms which are now part of the English language. It may be that this dictionary will not only help those who do not know what a particular foreign term means, but will sometimes surprise those who think they do know.

This dictionary defines the foreign words and expressions commonly used in English. Some words have ironic or other connotations and these are indicated (usually in parenthesis after the definition). Many terms have a specific context — law, art, music, etc — and this is noted, and, where appropriate, the historical origins of a word or phrase are discussed.

Pronunciation

The phonetic system used in this book is intended for use by the layman. It will be comprehensible to anyone with a reasonable command of English. Stresses are denoted by the capitalization of words, and syllables are indicated by hyphenation. Complete accuracy is impossible because many foreign vowel sounds cannot be translated perfectly into English. The best approximation would compel the addition of many symbols denoting long and short sounds, open and closed vowels, etc. We believe that such a system would make for confusion, rather than clarity, but each modern language section has a general guide to pronunciation. These aids to pronunciation will help the reader to give an accurate rendering of the phrase, but are no substitute for attempting to learn to read and speak the languages covered in this book.

How to Use This Book

Presentation

The phrase being defined is in **bold** type at the left of the page. Its pronunciation will be given in *italic* in brackets, followed by the definition.

Abbreviations used

abbr	abbreviated to
adj	adjectival use
adv	adverbial use
cf	compare with
colloq	colloquial
fig	figurative meaning
lit	literal meaning
n	noun
opp	opposite of
plu	plural
v	verb

Classical Languages

Nobody can underrate the importance of Latin in the formation of modern languages. It is the basis of Italian, Spanish, Portuguese, Catalan and Romanian, and of such less well-known tongues as Friulian and Rhaeto-Romansch. Through the other major Romance language, French, it has indirectly influenced even our own Germanic language, English. Latin, however, has been very much more than the root of language; it has also been the international language of learning, law and the Church. It is still the official language of the Roman Catholic Church and was abandoned as her liturgical language only in 1969. Up to the eighteenth century it was the language of scholars of all disciplines (Newton's *Principia* were written in Latin), and even in the early part of the present century doctoral theses at many European universities were presented in Latin. Thus a great many Latin words in all these language areas have simply become absorbed into the English language. It would be tedious (and outside the scope of this book) to attempt to list them all, but for the reader's interest we have placed words deriving from Classical mythology and history in Appendix 1.

The presence within a language of a foreign word or phrase is evidence of the cultural, political or technological dominance of that foreign country. Although the Romans became the masters of the Greek world, they drew a great deal of their culture from Greece. They modelled their poetry upon Greek forms and metres, they adopted the terms of Greek philosophy and rhetoric, and their medicine and their leading medical practitioners were also Greek. Thus such words as ode, chorus, epic, tragedy, comedy, antithesis, catharsis, apagoge, peripateia, periphrasis, phenomenon, phobia, scepsis, schema and stasis have passed unchanged from Greek into Latin and from Latin into English.

In the list of words and phrases which follows, the predominance of Latin may give a false impression of the real debt which the language owes to Greek. Latin was for so long the language of general education that those who wished to give the impression of being educated decorated their English with the Latin 'tag'. Greek however worked in the background providing the specialized and specific language of the sciences. To repay this debt and to guide readers to an understanding of these terms we have included selected Greek and Latin prefixes and suffixes (see Appendix 2 and Appendix 3).

Pronunciation

Although in Roman times there must have been a 'correct' way of pronouncing Latin, after the Decline and Fall, things went very much their own way and each nation has tended to give the Latin vowels and consonants the same values as its native language. The pronunciation system adopted here is the *classical* system, which is the most widely taught. This is an attempt by nineteenth-century philologists to establish an 'authentic' Roman pronunciation. Key features of this system are that *c*s are hard (pronounced like *k*), *j*s become *i*s and are pronounced like a *y* (hence *jus* becomes *ius*, pronounced *yus*), *v*s are pronounced like *w*s, *g*s are hard and all vowels are sounded (for example, *e* is not mute at the end of a word).

Presentation

The language from which the word or phrase is derived is given in italic in brackets, after the word being defined. *Lat* denotes Latin, *Gk* denotes Greek, and *Gk/Lat* indicates that a Greek word has passed into English through Latin.

A

a bene placito *(Lat)*   *(ah BEN-e PLAK-i-toh)* at pleasure

ab extra *(Lat)*   (ab EX-trah) from the outside

ab imo pectore*(Lat)*   *(ab EE-mo PEK-tor-ay)* from the bottom of the heart

ab initio *(Lat)*   *(ab in-I-tio)* from the beginning

ab origine *(Lat)*   *(ab or-REE-gin-AY)* from the outset

ab ovo *(Lat)*   *(ab OH-woh) lit:* from the egg; from the beginning

ab ovo usque ad mala *(Lat)*   *(ab OH-woh US-kwe ad MAH-la) lit:* from the egg to the apples; from beginning to end (Roman meals usually began with eggs and ended with apples)

absit invidia *(Lat)*   *(AB-sit in-WI-dia) lit:* may ill will be absent; no offence intended

absit omen *(Lat)*   *(AB-sit OH-men) lit:* may the omen be absent; God forbid

ab urbe condita *(Lat)*   *(ab URB-e KON-dit-ah)* from the foundation of the city (of Rome in 753 BC); the Roman method of dating (*abbr:* **AUC**)

abusus non tollit usum *(Lat)*   *(ab-USE-us non TOL-lit USE-um)* (in law) the dictum that the abuse of a right or privilege does not invalidate its use

academy   *see* Appendix 1

a capite ad calcem *(Lat)* (*a KAP-ee-tay ad KAL-kem*) *lit:* from head to heel; entirely, wholly

acedia *(Gk)* (*ah-KAY-dia*) listlessness, sloth

Achilles' heel *see* Appendix 1

acme *(Gk)* (*AK-mee*) culmination, point of perfection

acropolis *(Gk)* (*ak-RO-po-lis*) citadel, especially that of Athens

actaeon *see* Appendix 1

actum ne agas *(Lat)* (*AC-tum nay AG-ahs*) do not redo what has been done (*colloq:* get on with it)

AD *see* **anno Domini**

ad arbitrium *(Lat)* (*ad ahr-BIT-rium*) at will

ad astra *(Lat)* (*ad AST-ra*) to the stars, to the utmost

ad captandum vulgus *(Lat)* (*ad kap-TAND-um WUL-gus*) appealing to the emotions of the crowd

ad crumenam *(Lat)* (*ad CROO-men-am*) *lit:* to the purse; appealing to self-interest

ad fin *see* **ad finem**

ad finem *(Lat)* (*ad FEE-nem*) at the end of a page or text (*abbr:* **ad fin**)

ad hoc *(Lat)* (*ad HOK*) impromptu, improvised; for a specific occasion

ad hominem *(Lat)* (*ad HOM-in-em*) personal, relating to an individual; *see* **argumentum ad hominem**

ad infinitum *(Lat)* (*ad infee-NEE-tum*) endlessly, to infinity

ad lib *see* **ad libitum**

ad libitum *(Lat)* (*ad LIB-ee-tum*) *lit:* at pleasure; freely, extemporaneously (*abbr:* **ad lib**)

ad litem *(Lat)* *(ad LEE-tem)* (in law) guardian appointed to represent an infant

ad majorem Dei gloriam *(Lat)* *(ad mah-YOH-rem DE-ee GLOR-i-am)* to the greater glory of God; the motto of the Society of Jesus *(abbr:* **AMDG**)

ad misericordiam *(Lat)* *(ad mis-ER-i-CORD-i-am)* appealing to sympathy

ad modum *(Lat)* *(ad MO-dum)* in the manner of

ad nauseam *(Lat)* *(ad NAW-see-am)* to the point of sickness or disgust

adonis *see* Appendix 1

ad personam *(Lat)* *(ad per-SOH-nam)* personal, to the person, relating to the individual

ad rem *(Lat)* *(ad rem)* to the point, relevant to the matter under discussion, pertinent

adsum *(Lat)* *(ad-SUM) lit:* to be present; 'I am here', 'I am present' (answer to roll call)

ad unguem *(Lat)* *(ad UNG-wem) lit:* to the fingernail; precisely, to a nicety

ad unum omnes *(Lat)* *(ad OO-num OM-nes)* as one person, to a man

ad valorem *(Lat)* *(ad wal-OR-em)* according to the value (of goods, etc)

ad vitam aut culpam *(Lat)* *(ad WEE-tam owt CUL-pam)* (in law) allowing for good behaviour

advocatus diaboli *(Lat)* *(ad-woc-AH-tus di-A-bol-ee)* the devil's advocate

adynamia *(Gk)* *(ah-dai-NAM-ia)* absence of energy or force

aegis *see* Appendix 1

aegrotat *(Lat)* *(AI-groh-tat) lit:* he is ill, used of a certificate denoting illness (especially with reference to university degrees

	granted without examination)
aeolian	*see* Appendix 1
aes alienum *(Lat)*	*(AIS al-ee-AY-num) lit:* another's money; a debt
aesthesis *(Gk)*	*(ais-THAY-sis)* feeling, perception, sensitivity
aet/aetat *(Lat)*	*see* **aetatis**
aetatis *(Lat)*	*(AI-tah-tis)* aged, at the age of (*abbr:* **aet** and **aetat**)
a fortiori *(Lat)*	*(ah fort-ee-OR-i)* conclusively, with even stronger reason
agape *(Gk)*	*(AG-a-pay) lit:* fraternal devotion; the love of God for man; selfless Christian love
agon *(Gk)*	*(AG-ohn)* conflict, struggle, contest
agonippe *(Gk)*	*see* Appendix 1
agonistes *(Gk)*	*(a-gon-IS-tees)* contestant, one involved in conflict (especially mental conflict)
alma mater *(Lat)*	*(AL-ma MAH-ter) lit:* bounteous mother; beneficent or protective institution (usually with reference to school, college, etc)
alter *(Lat)*	*(AL-ter) lit:* another person; conception of the personality of another individual
alter ego *(Lat)*	*(AL-ter EH-go) lit:* one's second self; very close friend (often used inaccurately to mean another aspect of one's personality)
alter idem *(Lat)*	*(AL-ter EE-dem)* another precisely similar
alumni *(Lat)*	*see* **alumnus**
alumnus *(Lat)*	*(al-UM-nus)* student, learned person, graduate of an institution (*plu:* **alumni**)

am	*see* **ante meridiem**
a maximis ad minima *(Lat)*	*(ah MAX-i-mees ad MIN-i-ma)* from the largest to the smallest
amazon	*see* Appendix 1
ambrosia	*see* Appendix 1
AMDG	*see* **ad majorem Dei gloriam**
amicus curiae *(Lat)*	*(AM-ee-cus CUR-ee-ai) lit:* friend of the court; (in law) one who advises the court in a case not his own
amor patriae *(Lat)*	*(AM-or PAT-ri-ai)* patriotism, love of country
amor proximi *(Lat)*	*(AM-or PROX-i-mee)* love of one's neighbor
anathema sit *(Gk/Lat)*	*(an-A-them-a sit)* may he be accursed; pronouncement of excommunication (now used as a general exclamation)
anax andron *(Gk)*	*(AN-ax an-DROHN)* leader of men; a term Homer applied to Agamemnon and others
angulus terrarum *(Lat)*	*(ANG-u-lus ter-RAH-rum) lit:* quiet corner of the world; place where one feels most at home or comfortable, one's natural and favoured environment
anima *(Lat)*	*(AN-i-ma) lit:* mind, soul; inner self, true part of the personality; feminine part of man's personality. Jung contrasted the **anima** (true self) with the **persona** (assumed or externalized self)
animus furandi *(Lat)*	*(AN-i-mus fu-RAND-ee)* (in law) the intention of stealing
animus revocandi *(Lat)*	*(AN-i-mus ray-wok-AND-ee)* (in law) the intention of revoking a will or other contract
anni	*see* **annus**

anno *(Lat)* — *(AN-noh)* in the year of

anno aetatis suae *(Lat)* — *(AN-noh ai-TAH-tis SU-ai)* in the year of his age (*see* **aet**, **aetat** and **aetatis**)

anno Domini *(Lat)* — *(AN-noh DOM-in-ee)* in the year of our Lord, (from the first year) of the Christian era

anno regni *(Lat)* — *(AN-noh REG-nee)* in the year of the reign (of the present monarch)

annus *(Lat)* — *(AN-nus)* year (*plu:* **anni**)

annus mirabilis *(Lat)* — *(AN-nus mee-RAH-bil-is) lit:* wonderful year; remarkable year, year in which great and memorable events occurred

anomia — *see* **anomie**

anomie *(Gk)* — *(ah-NOM-ee)* condition of despair brought on by a breakdown in the rules of conduct and loss of sense of purpose (from **anomia**: lawlessness)

ante bellum *(Lat)* — *(AN-tay BEL-lum)* the period (and climate of opinion) before a war (especially the American Civil War)

ante litem motam *(Lat)* — *(AN-tay LEE-tem MOH-tam)* before litigation commenced, prior to the case coming to court

ante meridiem *(Lat)* — *(AN-tay mer-ID-ee-em)* in the morning, before midday (*abbr:* **am**)

apagoge *(Gk/Lat)* — *(ap-a-GOH-ge)* reduction to absurdity, indirect proof by demonstrating the falsity of the opposite point of view

aphrodisiac — *see* Appendix 1

apocalypsis *(Gk)* — *(ap-o-kal-IP-sis)* uncovering, revelation, disclosure

apocrypha *(Gk)* — *(ap-O-kri-fah) lit:* things which have been hidden; secrets, hidden things (especially applied to parts of the Bible which have been excluded from the authorized version

apollo   *see* Appendix 1

apologia *(Gk/Lat)*   *(apo-LOH-gia)* speech made in self-defence; the most famous example is the Apology of Socrates at his trial in 399 BC

apologia pro vita sua *(Lat)*   *(apo-LOH-gia proh WEET-ah SU-ah)* defence of his way of life; the title of Cardinal Newman's autobiography

a posse ad esse *(Lat)*   *(ah POS-se ad ES-se)* from the possible to the actual

a posteriori *(Lat)*   *(ah pos-TER-ri-o-ri)* (in logic) the reasoning from effects to causes, reasoning based on past experience (*opp:* **a priori**)

a primo *(Lat)*   *(ah PREE-moh)* from the first

a principio *(Lat)*   *(ah prin-KIP-i-oh)* from the beginning

a priori *(Lat)*   *(ah pri-OHR-ri)* (in logic) deductive reasoning, reasoning from causes to effects, ie without reference to experience (*opp*: **a posteriori**)

arbiter elegantiae *(Lat)*   *(AR-bit-er el-e-GANT-i-ai)* dictator of fashion, arbiter in matters of taste

arcadia   *see* Appendix 1

argumenti causa *(Lat)*   *(ar-gu-MEN-tee COW-sa)* for the sake of argument

argumentum ad crumenam *(Lat)*   *(ar-gu-MEN-tum ad CROO-men-am)* argument appealing to self-interest

argumentum ad ignorantiam *(Lat)*   *(ar-gu-MEN-tum ad ig-nor-ANT-i-am)* argument based on an adversary's ignorance

argumentum ad hominem *(Lat)*
(ar-gu-MEN-tum ad HOM-in-em) argument based on personal slander or praise which obscures the real points at issue

argumentum ad individium *(Lat)*
(ar-gu-MEN-tum ad in-di-WID-i-um) argument which appeals to men's prejudices

argumentum ad populum *(Lat)*
(ar-gu-MEN-tum ad POP-u-lum) argument appealing to the crowd

argumentum baculinum *(Lat)*
(ar-gu-MEN-tum BAK-u-LEE-num) argument dependent on physical force to sustain it

argumentum ex silentio *(Lat)*
(ar-gu-MEN-tum ex sil-ENT-i-oh) *lit:* argument out of silence; argument based on the absence of firm evidence

ariston metron *(Gk)*
(ar-IS-ton MET-ron) the middle course is the best; the golden mean should be pursued (Homer)

ars est celare artem *(Lat)*
(ars est kel-AHR-e ART-em) the true purpose of art is to conceal art

ars longa, vita brevis *(Lat)*
(ars LONG-a WEET-a BRE-wis) art is long, life is short (Seneca)

asbestos gelos *(Gk)*
(as-BEST-os GEL-os) inextinguishable laughter

ascesis *(Gk)*
(as-KAY-sis) the practice of self-discipline

ataraxia *(Gk)*
(ah-tar-AX-ia) calmness, inner contentment, passiveness; the serenity and indifference aimed at by the Stoics

ataxia *(Gk)*
(ah-TAX-ia) want of discipline, lack of order, absence of control of bodily functions

ate *(Gk)*
(AH-tay) infatuation, blindness of judgement sent by the gods (often used in a literary context)

atlas	*see* Appendix 1
AUC	*see* **ab urbe condita**
audentes fortuna iuvat *(Lat)*	*(ow-DENT-ays for-TOON-a yoo-vat)* fortune favours the daring (Virgil, *Aeneid*)
audita querela *(Lat)*	*(ow-DEE-ta KWER-eh-la)* (in law) writ giving leave to appeal
aurea mediocritas *(Lat)*	*(OW-re-a med-i-OK-rit-as)* the golden mean, the happy medium (axiom derived from Aristotle)
auri sacra fames *(Lat)*	*(OW-ree SAK-ra FAM-es)* (the) accursed lust for gold
aurora	*see* Appendix 1
auxilium ab alto *(Lat)*	*(owx-IL-i-um ab AL-toh)* help from on high
a vinculo matrimonii *(Lat)*	*(ah-VIN-cu-loh ma-tri-MON-ni-ee)* from the bond of matrimony

B

bacchic/ bacchanalian	*see* Appendix 1
bene decessit *(Lat)*	*(be-ne day-KESS-it) lit:* he has left well; statement that one's leaving of a situation is not due to misconduct or illwill
bene esse *(Lat)*	*(BE-ne ES-se)* well-being
bene merenti *(Lat)*	*(BE-ne mer-ENT-i)* (success) to those who deserve it
bene vobis *(Lat)*	*(BE-ne WOH-bis)* may you prosper
bona fide *(Lat)*	*(BON-ah FI-day) lit:* good faith; genuine, correct, legitimate
bona fides *(Lat)*	*(BON-ah FI-des)* documents proving identity or authority

bona vacantia
(Lat)
(BON-ah wak-ANT-ia) (in law) goods whose legal ownership is unknown

bonis avibus *(Lat)*
(BON-ees A-wi-bus) lit: with good birds (birds being a Roman means of divination); under good auspices

boreal
see Appendix 1

brutum fulmen
(Lat)
(BROO-tum FUL-men) ineffectual thunderbolt; (action which is) loud but ineffective

C

cachexia *(Gk)*
(kak-EX-ia) bad state of either body or mind

cacodaemon *(Gk)*
(kak-o-DAI-mohn) evil spirit, nightmare

cadmean/cadmeian
see Appendix 1

camera obscura
(Lat)
(KAM-er-a ob-SCOO-ra) lit: darkened room; box with an aperture and a sequence of mirrors by which an image is projected on to a screen (developed in the sixteenth century and the principle on which all cameras work)

caput mortuum
(Lat)
(KA-put MOR-too-um) residue left after distillation

carpe diem *(Lat)*
(KAR-pe DI-em) lit: seize the day, enjoy the day; take the opportunity while it is available

cassandra
see Appendix 1

casus belli *(Lat)*
(KAH-sus BEL-li) lit: case of war; grounds for a quarrel, occurrence giving rise to war

casus conscientiae
(Lat)
(KAH-sus KON-ski-ENT-ia) case of conscience

casus omissus *(Lat)* — *(KAH-sus om-IS-sus) lit:* case omitted; situation not envisaged by law, situation not covered by existing law

catachresis *(Gk)* — *(kat-a-KRAY-sis) lit:* against use; misapplication of a word

catastasis *(Gk)* — *(ka-ta-STA-sis)* (in drama) height or climax of the action

catharsis *(Gk)* — *(kath-AR-sis)* cleansing from guilt or defilement; purification; term used in tragic drama to indicate the period of suffering which expiates a sin

cathedra *(Gk)* — *(kath-HED-ra)* seat of authority

cathexis *(Gk)* — *(kath-EX-is)* burst of mental energy arising from a particular idea or object

causa movens *(Lat)* — *(KOW-sa MO-wens)* reason for undertaking a particular action

causa sine qua non *(Lat)* — *(KOW-sa si-ne kwah NON)* fundamental cause, necessary precondition (also used in English in the noun form **sine qua non**)

caveat *(Lat)* — *(KA-way-at) lit:* let him beware; caution, provision; (in law) the process whereby proceedings are halted

caveat emptor *(Lat)* — *(KA-way-at EMP-tor) lit:* let him beware; let the buyer beware (he alone is responsible for making a bad purchase)

cetera desunt *(Lat)* — *(KET-er-a day-SUNT) lit:* the rest is lacking; the text is incomplete (in literary scripts, official records, etc)

ceteris paribus *(Lat)* — *(KET-er-ees PAR-ri-bus)* other things being equal, if other conditions remain unchanged

charisma *(Gk)* — *(kar-IS-ma)* divinely conferred power; capacity to inspire enthusiasm and obedience in others; in Weber's terminology, the charismatic leader has

	innate qualities which give him the right to claim obedience
chimerical	*see* Appendix 1
clerici vagantes *(Lat)*	*(KLER-i-ki wa-GAHN-tes)* wandering scholars (the use of this term in English is largely sarcastic or ironic)
cogito ergo sum *(Lat)*	*(KOG-ee-toh ER-go SUM) lit:* I think therefore I am; assumption used by Descartes as the basis of his philosophical method
colossal	*see* Appendix 1
communi consensu *(Lat)*	*(kom-MOON-ee con-SEN-soo)* by common consent
compos mentis *(Lat)*	*(KOM-pos MEN-tis)* in a fit state of mind (*opp:* **non compos mentis**)
compos voti *(Lat)*	*(KOM-pos WOH-tee)* having obtained one's wish(es)
conscia mens recti *(Lat)*	*(KON-ski-a mens REK-tee)* (mind) conscious of being right
consensus facit legem *(Lat)*	*(kon-SEN-sus FAK-it LEG-um)* consent makes the law
contra bonos mores *(Lat)*	*(KON-tra BON-ohs MOHR-es)* contrary to sound morality
contra mundum *(Lat)*	*(KON-tra MUN-dum)* against the world; used primarily of one who takes an unpopular position and opposes majority feeling
corpus *(Lat)*	*(KOR-pus)* body, collection (of law, written works, etc)
corpus juris *(Lat)*	*(KOR-pus YOOR-is)* body of law
corrigenda	*see* **corrigendum**
corrigendum *(Lat)*	*(KOR-rig-END-um)* correction, something to be corrected (*plu:* **corrigenda**)

corruptio optimi pessima *(Lat)*
(cor-RUP-ti-oh OPT-i-mee PES-si-ma) when the best is corrupted it becomes the worst

cosmos *(Gk)*
(COS-mos) world or universe as an orderly and systematic whole

credo quia impossibile *(Lat)*
(KRAY-doh KWEE-a im-poss-IB-il-e) I believe because it is impossible; ie faith must sometimes supplant reason

crimen falsi *(Lat)*
(KREE-men FAL-see) lit: crime of falsification; perjury

cum grano salis *(Lat)*
(kum GRAH-noh SAL-ees) with a grain of salt; as in the English expression 'take it with a pinch of salt': do not be so gullible as to believe it all

cum notis variorum *(Lat)*
(kum NOH-tees WA-ri-OR-um) (classical texts) with the notes of various (critics)

cum privilegio *(Lat)*
(kum pri-vil-LEG-io) with privilege, with authority to print

curiosa felicitas *(Lat)*
(cur-i-OH-sa fay-LEE-ki-tas) painstaking spontaneity; term applied by Petronius to the verse of Horace, but true of all poets who succeed in the task of adapting the rhythms and language of everyday speech to the rhyme and metrical pattern of poetry

cursus honorum *(Lat)*
(KUR-sus hon-OR-um) lit: course of honours; sequence of posts leading to a high position; (in ancient Rome) the sequence of posts leading to Consul

D

daedalian/ daedalean
see Appendix 1

daemon *(Gk)*
(DAI-mohn) spirit holding rank midway between gods and men

damnosa haereditas *(Lat)*
(dam-NOH-sa hai-RED-i-tas) *lit:* inheritance of damnation; ruinous legacy

damnum sine injuria *(Lat)*
(DAM-num SEE-ne in-YOO-ri-ah) (in law) loss not subject to remedy, loss for which there can be no reparation

damoclean
see Appendix 1

decessit sine prole *(Lat)*
(de-KESS-it SEE-ne PRO-le) died without issue *(abbr:* **DSP**)

de facto *(Lat)*
(day FAK-toh) existing by fact, and not choice or right *(opp:* **de jure**)

de gustibus non est disputandum *(Lat)*
(day GUST-i-bus NOHN est DIS-put-AND-um) *lit:* in matters of taste, there is no (cause for) argument; each to his own taste

Dei gratia *(Lat)*
(DE-ee GRAH-ti-ah) by the grace of God

de integro *(Lat)*
(day in-TEG-roh) afresh, from the beginning again

de jure *(Lat)*
(day YOO-re) recognized as right and lawful *(opp:* **de facto**)

delineavit *(Lat)*
(DAY-lin-e-ah-wit) *lit:* he drew it; artist's signature on drawing, woodcut or engraving; *see* **sculpsit** and **excudit**

delirium tremens *(Lat)*
(day-LI-ri-um TRE-mens) alcoholic distress, with delusions and trembling

delphic
see Appendix 1

de minimis non curat lex *(Lat)*
(day MIN-i-mees non coo-rat lex) the law does not concern itself with trifles

de mortuis (nil nisi bonum) *(Lat)*
(day MOR-tu-ees nil ni-si BO-num) (say) nothing but good of the dead

demos *(Gk)*
(DAY-mos) the populace, the people; personification of the citizen body

demosthenic
see Appendix 1

Deo gratias *(Lat)*
(DE-oh GRAH-ti-ahs) thanks to God

Deo optimo maximo *(Lat)* — *(DE-oh OP-tim-oh MAX-i-moh)* for God, the best and the greatest; motto of the Benedictine order *(abbr:* **DOM**)

Deo volente *(Lat)* — *(DE-oh vol-EN-tay)* God willing (it will be achieved)

de profundis *(Lat)* — *(day pro-FUN-dees) lit:* from the depths; (arising) from extreme despair or anguish, the first words of the Latin version of Psalm 180, one of the seven penitential psalms

desiderata — *see* **desideratum**

desideratum *(Lat)* — *(day-SEED-er-AH-tum)* thing much desired or needed *(plu:* **desiderata**)

deus ex machina *(Lat)* — *(DE-us ex MAK-in-ah) lit:* god from a machine; being or device invoked to solve a particular problem otherwise insoluble; (in classical drama) the intervention of the gods to solve a problem: the 'god' was lowered on to the stage by means of a crane-like device

diathesis *(Gk)* — *(dai-a-THAY-sis)* arrangement of the composition in a work of art

dis aliter visum *(Lat)* — *(DEES AL-i-ter WEE-sum) lit:* the gods thought otherwise; used in explanation of same apparently inexplicable human failure

disjecta membra *(Lat)* — *(dis-YEK-ta MEM-bra) lit:* scattered limbs; disordered fragments of a work or task

dithyramb *(Gk)* — *(DI-thir-am)* Greek hymn of wild character; Bacchanalian song; any passionate or inflated writing or speech

DOM — *see* **Deo optimo maximo**

draconian *(Gk)* — *see* Appendix 1

dramatis personae *(dra-MAH-tis per-SOHN-ai) lit:*
(Lat) characters of a drama; list of characters
(in a literary work)

DSP *see* **decessit sine prole**

dum spiro, spero *(dum SPEE-roh SPE-roh)* while I
(Lat) breathe, I hope

dum vivimus, *dum wi-wi-mus wi-WAH-mus)* while
vivamus *(Lat)* we live, let us live (to the full)

durante bene *(dur-ANT-ay BE-ne PLAK-it-oh) lit:*
placito *(Lat)* during good pleasure; so long as the
authorities might wish

E

ecce homo *(Lat)* *(Ec-ce HO-moh) lit:* behold the man;
picture of Christ wearing a crown of
thorns

ecce signum *(Lat)* *(EC-ce SIG-num)* here is the proof

ecclesia *(Gk)* *(ek-LAY-sia)* general assembly (especially
of Athenian citizens)

e contra *(Lat)* *(ay CON-tra)* on the other hand, to take a
contrary position

editio princeps *(e-DIT-i-oh PRIN-keps)* first printed
(Lat) edition of a text

eg *see* **exempli gratia**

egeria *see* Appendix 1

ego *(Lat)* *(E-go) lit:* I, myself; (in psychology) an
individual's consciousness of himself

eirenicon *(Gk)* *(ay-RAY-NIK-on)* proposal outlining
terms of peace

elenchus *(Gk)* *(ay-LENG-kus)* logical refutation,
Socratic **elenchus:** mode of eliciting truth
by short question and answer sessions
used by Socrates

(empta dolore) experientia docet *(Lat)*	*(EMP-tah dol-OR-ay ex-peri-ENT-i-a DOK-et)* (painfully bought) experience teaches
en arche en ho logos	*see* **logos**
e necessitate *(Lat)*	*(AY ne-KESS-i-TAH-tay) lit:* from necessity; having no alternative; by force of circumstance
enosis *(Gk)*	*(e-NO-sis)* proposed political union between Cyprus and Greece (from Greek **henosis:** unity)
epanodos *(Gk)*	*(ep-ahn-OD-os)* recapitulation of the main points in a discourse
epea pteroenta *(Gk)*	*(EP-ay-a p'ter-o-EN-ta) lit:* winged words, significant statement (Homer)
epicurean	*see* Appendix 1
erebus	*see* Appendix 1
ergo *(Lat)*	*(ERR-goh)* therefore
erotic	*see* Appendix 1
errare est humanum *(Lat)*	*(err-AH-ray est hoo-MAH-num)* to err is human
et al	*see* **et alia**
et alia *(Lat)*	*(et AL-i-a)* and other things (*abbr:* **et al**, in which form it can also refer to people)
etc	*see* **et cetera**
et cetera *(Lat)*	*(et KET-te-ra) lit:* and the rest; and so forth (*abbr:* **etc**)
et hoc genus omne *(Lat)*	*(et HOK GEN-us OM-ne)* and all others of that sort; and others who are part of that group
et seq	*see* **et sequentes**
et sequentes *(Lat)*	*(et se-KWEN-tes)* and following (*abbr:* **et seq**)

et tu, Brute *(Lat)* — *(et too BROO-tay) lit:* you as well, Brutus; alleged exclamation of Caesar at the presence of Brutus among his assassins; exclamation of reproach at an act of treachery committed by a close friend

etymon *(Gk)* — *(ET-i-mohn)* original form of a word; the literal sense

eureka *(Gk)* — *(yew-REE-kah) lit:* true, real, genuine; 'I have found it'; phrase used by Archimedes on discovering the principle of water displacement

ex cathedra *(Gk/Lat)* — *(ex kath-HED-ra) lit:* from seat; from a position of authority, official

exceptio probat regulam *(Lat)* — *(ex KEP-ti-oh prob-at REG-u-lam)* it is the exception which proves the rule

exceptis excipiendis *(Lat)* — *(ex-KEP-tees ex-kip-i-END-ees) lit:* things excluded which should be excluded; taking the necessary exceptions into account

excudit *(Lat)* — *(ex KOO-dit) lit:* he cast (it); artist's signature on bronze statues, medals, etc

ex curia *(Lat)* — *(ex coo-ri-ah)* out of court

ex delicto *(Lat)* — *(ex day-LIK-toh)* (in law) a matter arising out of a crime

ex dono *(Lat)* — *(ex DOH-noh)* by gift of, donated by

exeat *(Lat)* — *(EX-ay-at) lit:* he may go out; formula allowing a pupil to be absent from school

exempli gratia *(Lat)* — *(ex-EM-plee GRAH-ti-ah)* for example *(abbr:* **eg)**

ex gratia *(Lat)* — *(ex GRAH-ti-ah)* (performed) as an act of grace, (an action) carried out by choice not necessity

ex libris *(Lat)* — *(ex LIB-rees)* from the library of; used on bookplates to identify ownership

ex nihilo *(Lat)* — *(ex NI-hil-oh)* from nothing

ex nihilo nihil fit *(Lat)* — *(ex NI-hil-oh NI-hil fit)* from nothing, nothing can be made

ex officio *(Lat)* — *(ex of-FIK-ee-oh)* by virtue of an office held, (sitting on committee, etc) because of office held

ex parte *(Lat)* — *(ex PAR-tay) lit:* from one side; partisan, for one side only (usually used in law)

ex pede Herculem *(Lat)* — *(ex PED-e HER-cu-lem) lit:* (to measure) Hercules from his foot; to estimate the size or extent of the unknown whole from the known part

experientia docet — *see* **(empta dolore) experientia docet**

experto credite *(Lat)* — *(ex-PER-toh KRED-i-tay)* trust in one who has experience

ex post facto *(Lat)* — *(ex post FAK-toh)* after the fact, retrospectively; by reason of something having been done afterwards

ex tempore *(Lat)* — *(ex TEM-por-AY) lit:* out of the time; without preparation, spontaneously

ex voto *(Lat)* — *(ex WOH-toh) lit:* out of a vow; (offering made) in pursuance of a vow; often a painting or sculpture dedicated to one's church

F

f — *see* **fecit**

faber est quisque fortunae suae *(Lat)* — *(FAB-er est kwis-kwe for-TOON-ai SU-ai)* (every) man is the architect of his own fortune

facta non verba *(Lat)* — *(FAK-ta nohn WER-ba) lit:* deeds not words; (what is required is) action not speeches

factotum *(Lat)* — *(fak-TOH-tum)* one who does everything; general dogsbody, manservant

fascia *(Lat)* — *(FAS-ki-a) lit:* band, strip; horizontal plane of wood or stone under cornice

fec — *see* **fecit**

fecit *(Lat)* — *(FAY-kit) lit:* he has made, made by; general attribution of artistic authorship, engraving, etc *(abbr:* **f** or **fec**)

felix qui potuit rerum cognoscere causas *(Lat)* — *(FAY-lix kwee POT-u-it REHR-um kog-NOS-ker-e COW-sas)* fortunate is the man who understands the causes of things

ferae naturae *(Lat)* — *(fer-AI nat-OOR-ai)* uncivilized, undomesticated beasts

festina lente *(Lat)* — *(FES-teen-ah LEN-te)* more haste, less speed; *see* **spende bradeos**

fiat justitia, ruat caelum *(Lat)* — *(FEE-at yus-TIT-i-a RU-at KAI-lum)* let justice be done, though the heavens fall in ruin

fidei defensor *(Lat)* — *(fid-E-i day-FEN-sor)* defender of the faith; title attributed to the sovereign and inscribed on coins

fidus Achates *(Lat)* — *(FEE-dus ak-AH-tees)* faithful companion; Achates was the faithful comrade of Aeneas

fieri facias *(Lat)* — *(fee-EH-ri FAK-ias) lit:* you may make it happen; (in law) a writ authorizing a sheriff to distrain the defendant's goods

(in) flagrante delicto *(Lat)* — *(in flag-RAN-tay day-LIK-toh) lit:* in the heat of the crime; in the act, in compromising circumstances

florilegium *(Lat)* — *(flor-i-LEHG-ium) lit:* bunch of flowers; anthology, collection

floruit *(Lat)* | *(FLOR-oo-it) lit:* he flourished; flourishing, zenith; the period during which a person reached the peak of his career, produced his greatest works, etc

fortuna favet fortibus *(Lat)* | *(for-TOO-na FA-vet FOR-ti-bus)* fortune favours the strong

fortuna nulla fides frontis *(Lat)* | *(for-TOO-na noo-la FEE-des FRUN-tis)* do not trust in appearance; appearances are likely to deceive (Juvenal)

furies | *see* Appendix 1

G

ganymedes | *see* Appendix 1

gaudium certaminis *(Lat)* | *(GOW-dium ker-TAH-min-is)* the joy of the struggle

genius loci *(Lat)* | *(GEN-i-us LO-ki)* atmosphere, prevailing character, spirit of a place

genus *(Lat)* | *(GE-nus)* class of things sharing certain attributes, group of related species

gnome *(Gk)* | *(GNOH-may)* maxim, aphorism

gnosis *(Gk)* | *(GNOH-sis)* knowledge, understanding, especially of spiritual mysteries

gnothi seauton *(Gk)* | *(GNOH-thi se-OW-ton)* know thyself; this maxim was written over the door of the Delphic Oracle and taken up by the Sophists

gordian | *see* Appendix 1

gratis *(Lat)* | *(GRAH-tees) lit:* for nothing; without reward, free, gratuitous

gratis dictum *(Lat)* | *(GRAH-tees DIK-tum)* vacuous assertion, glib statement

H

habeas corpus *(Lat)*

(HAB-ay-as COR-pus) writ requiring the appearance of a prisoner in court to determine the legality of his detention; crucial tenet of British justice, introduced by the Habeas Corpus Act of 1679, which does not allow the police to hold a person for more than a short period without a court deciding that his detention is justified

halcyon *(Gk)*

(HAL-see-on) lit: kingfisher; *adj:* calm, peaceful; the kingfisher was reputed to breed in floating nests on sea and to charm wind and sea into calm for the purpose

hamartia *(Gk)*

(ham-ART-ia) failure, tragic flaw, defect of character which brings disaster upon its bearer

hebdomad *(Gk)*

(HEB-do-mad) seven days, a week

hebe

see Appendix 1

heliconian

see Appendix 1

henosis

see **enosis**

herculean

see Appendix 1

hic sepultus *(Lat)*

(HEEK se-PULT-us) here (lies) buried

hinc illae lacrimae *(Lat)*

(HINC IL-lai LAK-rim-ai) lit: hence these tears; this was the cause of the disaster

hippocratic

see Appendix 1

hoi polloi *(Gk)*

(HOI poll-OI) the many, the rabble

homo homini lupus *(Lat)*

(HOH-mo HOM-in-ee LOO-pus) man (is) a wolf to his fellow man

homo nullius coloris *(Lat)*

(HOH-mo NULL-i-us col-OR-is) lit: man of no colour; one who does not commit

himself (to an argument, position, etc)

homo rationalis *(Lat)*
(HOH-mo ra-shon-AL-is) lit: rational man; notion of man as a cognitive being

homo sapiens *(Lat)*
(HOH-mo SAYP-iens) rational man, member of the human species

homo unius libri *(Lat)*
(HOH-mo OON-ius LEE-bri) lit: man of one book; obscurantist, partisan; used disparagingly to indicate a man versed in only one text

homunculus *(Lat)*
(hoh-MUN-kew-lus) miniature man; often depicted as residing within an individual and influencing his judgement and action

honoris causa *(Lat)*
(hon-OR-is COW-sa) lit: for the sake of honour; (often) degree conferred without examination in recognition of some particular achievement

hora fugit *(Lat)*
lit: time flies; time passes quickly (*see* **tempus fugit**)

horribile dictu *(Lat)*
horrible to tell, terrible to relate (*cf* **mirabile dictu**)

hubris *(Gk)*
(HUB-ris) insolent or overweening pride leading to disaster; (in Greek tragedy) a refusal to accept the authority of the gods, leading to disaster

humani generis *(Lat)*
(hoo-MAH-ni GEN-er-is) lit: of the human race; title of an encyclical issued by Pope Pius XII attacking Christian existentialism and its attempts to rationalize Christian thought

humanitas *(Lat)*
(hoo-MAH-ni-tas) the study of the liberal arts; an educated approach to human affairs

hydra
see Appendix 1

hyperborean
see Appendix 1

I

ibid   *see* **ibidem**

ibidem *(Lat)*   *(ib-ee-dem) lit:* the same; (used in citation to indicate) occurring in the same text (*abbr:* **ibid**)

id *(Lat)*   *(id) lit:* that; (in psychology) the fund of unconscious energies and impulses which motivate an individual

id est *(Lat)*   (id est) that is *(abbr:* **ie**)

ignorantia legis neminem excusat *(Lat)*   *(ig-nor-AHN-ti-a LAY-gis NEM-in-em ex-COO-sat)* ignorance of the law is not an excuse

ignorantio legis non exculpat *(Lat)*   *(ig-nor-AHN-ti-oh LAY-gis NOHN ex-CUL-pat)* to be ignorant of the law does not excuse (a misdemeanour)

ignoratio elenchi *(Lat)*   *(ig-nor-AH-ti-oh ay-LENG-ki)* irrelevant argument; (in logic) the fallacy of refuting an irrelevant proposition, ignoring the point at issue

IHS   *see* **in hoc signo**

iliad   *see* Appendix 1

imago pietatis *(Lat)*   *(im-AH-goh PEE-ay-TAH-tis) lit:* image of piety; representation in religious art of the dead Christ standing upright in his tomb

imo pectore *(Lat)*   *(EEM-oh PEK-tor-ay)* from (in) the innermost recesses of the heart

impari marte *(Lat)*   *(im-PAR-i MAR-tay)* in unequal combat

imprimatur *(Lat)*   *(im-preem-AH-tur)* official sanction for the publication of a text (especially papal authority for encyclical)

in absentia *(Lat)*   *(in ab-SEN-ti-ah)* in the absence of the person concerned

in aeternum *(Lat)*	*(in ai-TER-num)* forever, eternally
in camera *(Lat)*	*(in KAM-er-ah) lit:* in a room; proceedings conducted in secret (usually with reference to legal cases thus conducted)
incipit *(Lat)*	*(in-KIP-it)* the beginning of a text (usually the first few words)
in contumaciam *(Lat)*	*(in kon-tum-AH-ki-am)* (in law) in contempt (of court)
incunabula *(Lat)*	*(in-koon-AH-bu-la)* the earliest printed books (ie those printed before about 1500)
incunabulum *(Lat)*	*(in-koon-AH-bu-lum) lit:* swaddling clothes; infancy, origin; the birthplace, origin (of a movement)
in discrimine rerum *(Lat)*	*(in-dis-CRIM-in-ay REHR-um)* at the crisis point (of affairs), at the turning point
in excelsis *(Lat)*	*(in ex-CEL-sees)* in the highest, in the greatest measure
in extenso *(Lat)*	*(in ex-TEN-soh)* in its entirety, completely
in extremis *(Lat)*	*(in ex-TRAY-mees)* on the point of death, at the extremity (usually of suffering)
infra dig(nitatem) *(Lat)*	*(IN-fra dig-ni-TAH-tem)* beneath one's dignity
in hoc signo *(Lat)*	*(in HOK SIG-noh)* in this sign (ie the Cross); motto of the Jesuits
in hoc signo vinces *(Lat)*	*(in HOK SIG-noh WIN-kes)* in this sign you will conquer; motto of the Emperor Constantine
in limine *(Lat)*	*(in LIM-i-nay)* at the outset

in loco citato *(Lat)*   *(in LOH-coh kit-AH-toh)* occurring in the place (book, document, etc) cited (*abbr:* **loc cit**)

in loco parentis *(Lat)*   *(in LOH-coh pah-REN-tis)* in the place of the parent

in medias res *(Lat)*   *(in MED-i-as RAYS)* in the middle, in the midst of affairs

in memoriam *(Lat)*   *(in mem-OR-i-am)* in memory of; document, notice, etc in memory of a deceased person

in nomine *(Lat)*   *(in NOM-in-ay)* in the name of

in nuce *(Lat)*   *(in NUK-e)* in a nutshell, put succinctly

in personam *(Lat)*   *(in per-SOH-nam)* (legal action taken) against the person, against the individual (*cf* **in rem**)

in posse *(Lat)*   *(in POSS-e) lit:* as a possibility; potentially

in principio *(Lat)*   *(in prin-KIP-ee-oh)* in the beginning, at the outset

in puris naturalibus *(Lat)*   *(in POOH-rees na-toor-AH-li-bus)* in the natural state, naked

in re *(Lat)*   *(in RAY)* in the matter of (*plu:* **in rebus**)

in rebus   *see* **in rem**

in rem *(Lat)*   *(in REM) lit:* against the matter, against the thing; (in law) when action is taken against contraband goods, etc (*cf* **in personam**)

in situ *(Lat)*   *(in SIT-oo)* in its original place; in its appointed place; in its usual environment

in statu pupillari *(Lat)*   *(in STA-too pooh-pil-LAHR-ee)* having the status of a student

in statu quo ante *(Lat)*   *(in STA-too kwoh AN-tay)* in the same condition as before, unchanged

in tenebris *(Lat)* — *(in TEN-e-brees)* in darkness, incomprehensible, obscure

inter alia *(Lat)* — *(IN-ter AL-i-a)* among other things; *see* **inter alios**

inter alios *(Lat)* — *(IN-ter AL-i-ohs)* among other persons

inter partes *(Lat)* — *(IN-ter PAR-tes)* (in law) with both sides represented

in toto *(Lat)* — *(in TOH-toh)* as a whole, in its entirety, completely

in transitu *(Lat)* — *(in TRAN-sit-oo)* in transit, in passage

intra vires *(Lat)* — *(IN-tra WI-res)* within one's jurisdication or authority (*opp:* **ultra vires**)

in vino veritas *(Lat)* — *(in WEE-noh WER-i-tas) lit:* in wine there is truth; one speaks freely under the influence of drink

iota *(Gk)* — *(ai-OH-ta)* Greek letter i; atom, jot

ipse dixit *(Lat)* — *(IP-se DIX-it) lit:* he himself said it; unsubstantiated and dogmatic assertion that has no authority

ipsissima verba *(Lat)* — *(ip-SEES-si-ma WER-ba)* (quoted) in the exact words

ipso facto *(Lat)* — *(IP-soh FAK-toh)* by the fact itself, intrinsically

ipso jure *(Lat)* — *(IP-soh YOOR-e)* by law, by judgement

item *(Lat)* — *(EE-tem)* also, similarly (used in listing or cataloguing things)

J

jacta alea est *(Lat)* — *(YAK-ta AL-e-a est) lit:* the die is cast; exclamation of Caesar on crossing the Rubicon in 49 BC, effectively the beginning of his war with Pompey

jus contra bellum *(Lat)* — *(YUS CON-tra BEL-lum) lit:* law against war; the 'moral' law which makes all warmongering unjust

jus gentium *(Lat)* — *(YUS GEN-ti-um)* international law; law prevailing among nations

jus in bello *(Lat)* — *(YUS in BEL-loh) lit:* law in war; the notion that even the state of war has moral constraints and conventions which must be obeyed

juvenilia *(Lat)* — *(yoo-wen-EE-li-a)* collection of youthful works; collective term for the immature output of writer

K

kalos kagathos *(Gk)* — *(KAH-los KAHG-a-thos)* the good and beautiful; a gentleman

ktema es aei *(Gk)* — *(K'TAY-ma es ai)* a possession forever; Thucydides describing his book on the Peloponnesian war

kudos *(Gk)* — *(KEW-dos)* glory, renown, fame

L

laborare est orare *(Lat)* — *(la-boh-rah-re est oh-rah-re)* to work is to pray

laconic — *see* Appendix I

lacuna *(Lat)* — *(la-COO-na)* gap, blank space, cavity, hiatus, missing part of text, etc (*plu:* **lacunae**)

lacunae — *see* **lacuna**

laesa majestas *(Lat)* — *(LAI-sa mai-YES-tas)* (the crime of) high treason

lapsus calami *(Lat)* — *(LAP-sus CAL-a-mee)* slip of the pen

lapsus linguae *(Lat)* — *(LAP-sus LING-wai)* slip of the tongue

lapsus memoriae *(Lat)* — *(LAP-sus mem-OR-i-AI)* lapse or fault of memory

laudator temporis acti *(Lat)* — *(low-DAH-tor tem-POR-is AK-ti) lit:* praiser of past times; one who prefers the past to the present

lector benevole *(Lat)* — *(LEK-tor be-ne-VO-le) lit:* kind reader; common opening of an author's preface

legatus a latere *(Lat)* — *(le-GAH-tus ah LAT-e-re) lit:* ambassador from the inner circle; the formal description of a papal legate

lemma *(Gk)* — *(LAY-ma)* assumed or demonstrated proposition used in argument or proof

lethean — *see* Appendix 1

lex domicilii *(Lat)* — *(lex dom-i-KILL-ee-ee)* the law in force at one's place of domicile (in divorce cases, etc)

lex non scripta *(Lat)* — *(lex nohn-SCRIP-ta) lit:* law which has not been written or recorded, customary law, common law

lex scripta *(Lat)* — *(lex SCRIP-ta) lit:* written law; statute law

lex talionis *(Lat)* — *(lex tal-i-OH-nis)* the law of retribution (allowing a victim to retaliate)

libido *(Lat)* — *(lib-EE-doh) lit:* lust; sexual drive; (in psychology) usually applied to sexual impulse, but may be applied to all motivations

lite pendente *(Lat)* — *(LEE-tay pen-DEN-tay)* while the case is pending

loc cit — *see* in loco citato

locus classicus *(Lat)* — *(LO-cus CLAS-sic-us)* standard source of an idea or reference, most important reference, most authoritative passage (on a subject)

locus communis *(Lat)* — *(LO-cus com-MUNE-is)* a commonplace, passage often quoted (often carrying the connotation of cliché)

locus standi *(Lat)* — *(LO-cus STAN-dee)* *lit:* place to stand; recognized position; right to intervene, right to appear in court, etc

logos *(Gk)* — *(LO-gos)* word, reason, argument; (in theology) the Word (eg in St John's Gospel: **en arche en ho logos** — in the beginning was the Word)

lotus — *see* Appendix 1

lusus naturae *(Lat)* — *(LOO-sus NAT-oor-ai)* freak of nature, highly unusual natural occurrence

lyceum — *see* Appendix 1

M

magna cum laude *(Lat)* — *(MAG-na coom LOW-day)* with much distinction, with high honours

magni nominis umbra *(Lat)* — *(MAG-nee NOM-i-nis UMB-ra)* the shadow of a mighty name

magnum opus *(Lat)* — *(MAG-num OP-us)* most important work, work of great scale or stature; (writer's, artist's) greatest work

maleficium *(Lat)* — *(mal-eh-FICK-ium)* evil deed, crime

marathon — *see* Appendix 1

mare *(Lat)* — *(MAH-re)* *lit:* sea; now applied to the 'seas' on the moon and Mars (dark patches once thought to contain water)

mare clausum *(Lat)* — *(MAR-re CLOW-sum)* *lit:* closed sea; sea within the jurisdiction of one state

mare nostrum *(Lat)* — *(MAH-re NOS-trum)* *lit:* our sea; the Meditteranean

martial — *see* Appendix 1

mea culpa *(Lat)* — *(ME-a CUL-pa) lit:* I am guilty; admission of guilt

meden agan *(Gk)* — *(MAY-den AG-ahn)* nothing in excess; (there is virtue) in moderation

medusa — *see* Appendix 1

me judice *(Lat)* — *(MAY YOO-di-kay)* in my judgement

memento mori *(Lat)* — *(me-MEN-toh MO-ri) lit:* reminder of death; remember that you must die

mens sana in corpore sano *(Lat)* — *(MENS SAH-na in COR-por-e SAH-noh)* a healthy mind (will exist) in a healthy body

mentor — *see* Appendix 1

meo periculo *(Lat)* — *(me-oh per-IK-ul-oh)* at my risk

mercurial — *see* Appendix 1

mirabile dictu *(Lat)* — *(mee-RAH-bee-lay DIK-tu) lit:* marvellous to say; wonderful to relate (*cf* **horrible dictu**)

mittimus *(Lat)* — *(MIT-ti-mus)* (in law) writ ordering the keeper of a prison to receive a person into custody

mobile vulgus *(Lat)* — *(MOH-bil-e WUL-gus)* (the) fickle crowd

modus docendi *(Lat)* — *(MO-dus dok-END-ee)* method of teaching

modus loquendi *(Lat)* — *(MO-dus lok-WEND-ee)* way of speaking, style of speech

modus operandi *(Lat)* — *(MO-dus OP-er-AND-ee)* method of operation

modus vivendi *(Lat)* — *(MO-dus wee-WEN-dee) lit:* mode of living; working arrangment in a situation where two parties are at odds with one another

mores *(Lat)* — *(MOR-es)* conduct, morals, customs (usually of country, society, etc) (plural of mos: custom)

more suo *(Lat)*   *(MOR-e SU-oh)* in his own manner, fashion, habit, etc

morphine   *see* Appendix 1

mos maiorum *(Lat)*   *(mohs mai-OR-um)* the custom of one's ancestors; established practice

motu proprio *(Lat)*   *(MOH-too PROP-ri-oh)* of one's own impulsion, (acting) on one's own initiative

muse   *see* Appendix 1

mutatis mutandis *(Lat)*   *(moo-TAH-tees moo-TAND-ees) lit:* things having been changed which should be changed; allowing for the appropriate changes

mutato nomine *(Lat)*   *(moo-TAH-toh NOM-in-e)* under a different name

myrmidon   *see* Appendix 1

N

narcissism   *see* Appendix 1

natura abhorret vacuum *(Lat)*   *(nat-OOR-a AB-hor-re WAC-u-um)* nature abhors a vacuum (Descartes)

nb   *see* **nota bene**

necessitas non habet legem *(Lat)*   *(nek-ES-si-tas nohn HAB-et LEG-em) lit:* necessity has no law; notion that in certain situations moral codes break down completely

nectar   *see* Appendix 1

nem con   *see* **nemini contradicente**

nemesis   *see* Appendix 1

nemini contradicente *(Lat)*   *(NE-mi-nee con-tra-dik-ENT-e) lit:* nobody dissenting; without opposition, unanimous; usually describes the passage of a resolution in a debate (*abbr:* **nem con**)

ne plus ultra *(Lat)* *(nay ploos UL-tra) lit:* nothing more beyond; no further beyond, furthest point attainable, acme, highest point, obstacle to further advance

nestor *see* **Appendix 1**

nihil ad rem *(Lat)* *(ni-hil ad rem) lit:* nothing to the matter (in hand); irrelevant

nihil ex nihilo fit *(Lat)* *(ni-hil ex nil-EE-oh fit) lit:* nothing comes from nothing; the argument from first cause, ie that matter must have been created by a divine force

nihil obstat *(Lat)* *(ni-hil OB-stat) lit:* nothing hinders; statement from a censor that a text contains nothing which hinders its printing or production

nil admirari *(Lat)* *(nil ad-meer-AHR-i) lit:* nothing surprises; (state of) perfect composure and equanimity

nil desperandum *(Lat)* *(nil DAY-spay-RAND-um)* do not despair; no reason to despair

niobe *see* Appendix 1

nolle prosequi *(Lat)* *(NOL-le pro-SEK-wee)* (in law) statement that a prosecutor does not wish to further his suit; writ ending court proceedings because there is no case to answer

nolo episcopari *(Lat)* *(NOH-loh e-pis-kop-AHR-ee) lit:* I do not wish to serve; the formula for the refusal of any honour or office

non compos mentis *(Lat)* *(nohn COM-pos MEN-tis) lit:* not in control of one's mind; deranged, insane

non est factum *(Lat)* *(nohn est FAK-tum) lit:* it is not done; (in law) principle that a party to a contract is not bound by its terms because he did not understand its provisions

non omnis moriar *(Lat)* — *(nohn OM-nis MOR-ee-ahr) lit:* I shall not die entirely something will live after me; I leave something for posterity

non placet *(Lat)* — *(nohn PLAK-et) lit:* it does not please (me); the formula for giving a negative vote (in Church synods, university assemblies, etc)

non sequitur *(Lat)* — *(nohn SEK-wi-tur) lit:* it does not follow; something which does not follow from that expressed immediately before

nostrum *(Lat)* — *(NOS-trum) lit:* our own; patent medicine (or scheme)

nota bene *(Lat)* — *(NOH-ta BE-ne) lit:* note well; take note of what follows (usually a qualification to something that has gone before)

nulli secundus *(Lat)* — *(NUL-lee se-KUN-dus)* second to none

O

obiit sine prole *(Lat)* — *(OB-ee-it si-ne PROH-le)* died without issue (*abbr:* **OSP**)

obiter dicta — *see* **obiter dictum**

obiter dictum *(Lat)* — *(OH-bi-ter DICK-tum)* incidental remark; (in law) a remark by the judge which is outside the content of his judgement (*plu:* **obiter dicta**)

obscurum per obscurius *(Lat)* — *(ob-SCOO-rum per ob-SCOO-rius)* explanation of something obscure by means of something even more obscure

occasio facit furem *(Lat)* — *(ok-KAH-si-oh FAK-it FOO-rem)* (the) occasion makes the thief

oderint dum metuant *(Lat)* — *(OH-der-int dum MET-u-ant)* let them hate me, as long as they fear me

odium scholasticum *(Lat)* — *(OD-i-um sko-LAS-ti-kum)* the acrimony of pedants and scholars; academic quibbling over minor points of detail

odyssey	*see* Appendix 1
oedipus	*see* Appendix 1
olet lucernam	*(OL-et loo-KER-nam) lit:* it smells of the lamp; laboured piece of writing which betrays the effort and pedantry put into it
olympiad	*see* Appendix 1
olympian	*see* Appendix 1
omega *(Gk)*	*(OH-me-ga)* last letter of the Greek alphabet; last of series
omne vivum ex vivo *(Lat)*	*(OM-ne WEE-WUM ex WEE-woh) lit:* every living thing from a living thing; assertion that nothing can be spontaneously created, ie that all living things are descended from other living things
omnia vincit amor *(Lat)*	*(OM-ne-ah WIN-kit AH-mor)* love conquers all (things)
omphalus *(Gk)*	*(OM-fal-us)* boss on shield; conical stone at Delphi supposed to be the central point of the earth, central line
op	*see* **opus**
op cit	*see* **opere citato**
opera	*see* **opus**
opere citato *(Lat)*	*(OP-er-e kit-AH-toh)* (occurring) in the work cited (*abbr:* **op cit**)
optimates *(Lat)*	*(op-ti-MAH-tays)* the aristocracy, the best people (often employed ironically or sarcastically)
opus *(Lat)*	*(OP-us)* work, musical composition (*abbr:* **op**); a composer's works are usually arranged chronologically and given an opus number (*plu:* **opera**)
oratio obliqua *(Lat)*	*(or-AH-tio ob-LEE-kwa)* second-hand reports, hearsay

orphic/orphean *see* Appendix 1

O si sic omnes
(Lat) *(OH see seek OM-nes)* if only everyone were like that

OSP *see* **obiit sine prole**

**O tempora, O
mores** *(Lat)* *(OH TEM-por-a OH-mor-ays) lit:* oh, the times! oh, the manners!; exclamation suggesting dissatisfaction with changing times, changing values, etc (derived from Cicero)

oxygian *see* Appendix 1

P

p *see* **pinxit**

pace *(Lat)* *(PAH-ke)* by grace of, in deference to; often used when the locutor is disagreeing with a respected authority, but may also be used ironically

palladium *see* Appendix 1

Pandora's box *see* Appendix 1

panta rhei *(Gk)* *(PAN-ta ray)* everything is in a state of flux (Heraclitus)

**panton anthropon
metron einai** *(Gk)* *(PAN-tohn AN-throh-pon MET-ron AY-nai)* man is the measure of all things (Protagoras, quoted by Plato)

papyrus *(Gk)* *(pap-i-rus)* paper reed; ancient writing material prepared by Egyptians

pari passu *(Lat)* *(PAR-i PAH-soo) lit:* with equal pace; side by side, equitably

paterfamilias *(Lat)* *(PA-ter-fam-EE-lias)* head of family

pater patriae *(Lat)* *(PA-ter PAT-ri-ai)* (the) father of his country; title assumed by Augustus and the Emperors who followed him

patres conscripti
(Lat) *(PA-trays con-SCRIP-tee) lit:* fathers of the list; the Roman senators

pax Britannica *(Lat)* — *(PAX brit-AN-ni-ca)* British peace, the area where British law and authority was sovereign

pax Romana *(Lat)* — *(PAX ro-MA-nah)* the area over which Roman law and authority was sovereign

pax vobiscum *(Lat)* — *(PAX woh-BIS-cum)* peace (be) with you

peccavi *(Lat)* — *(pek-KAH-wee)* *lit:* I have sinned; to admit to being in the wrong

per annum *(Lat)* — *(per AN-num)* annually, per year

per ardua ad astra *(Lat)* — *(per ARD-u-a ad AS-tra)* through adversity to reach the stars; the motto of the Royal Air Force

per capita — *see* **per caput**

per caput *(Lat)* — *(per KAP-ut)* by head (of population), for each person (*abbr:* **per capita**, in which form it is used adjectivally — **per capita** productivity, etc)

per contra *(Lat)* — *(per KON-tra)* on the other hand, to take a contrary position

per diem *(Lat)* — *(per DI-em)* per day, each day

perfervidum ingenium *(Lat)* — *(per-fer-WID-um in GEN-ium)* extreme ardour or enthusiasm

peripateia *(Gk)* — *(per-i-pat-AY-ee-a)* *lit:* turning point; sudden change of fortune (especially in theatrical drama)

perpetuum mobile *(Lat)* — *(per PET-u-um MOH-bil-e)* perpetual motion

per procurationem *(Lat)* — *(per PROH-coor-AH-ti-oh-nem)* by the action of an appointed agent (*abbr:* **pp**, as in the case of a letter signed by a secretary or assistant)

per se *(Lat)* — *(per say)* by itself, inherently

persona *(Lat)*

(per-SOH-na) person, character, role; (in psychology) outward personality; attributes of personality transmitted to others (*cf* **anima**)

persona grata *(Lat)*

(per-SOH-na GRAH-ta) welcome person, acceptable person (*opp:* **persona non grata**)

persona non grata *(Lat)*

(per-SOH-na nohn GRAH-ta) lit: person not welcome; an unacceptable person (*opp:* **persona grata**)

petitio principii *(Lat)*

(peh-TEE-ti-oh PRIN-ki-pi-ee) (in logic and law) begging the question

phagomen kai piomen, aurion gar thanoumetha *(Gk)*

(fag-OH-men kai pi-OH-men OW-ri-on gar than-OO-meth-a) let us eat and drink, for tomorrow we die — dictum of Epicurus of Samos, d 270 BC, who argued that peace of mind is achieved through the absence of fear, and that the sources of fear are religion and death; hence the notion of living for the moment, which has led to epicureanism being confused with hedonism

pinxit *(Lat)*

(PINX-it) lit: he painted it; painted by; attribution of authorship to a painting, drawing, engraving, etc (*abbr:* **p**)

placet *(Lat)*

(PLAK-et) the formula for giving an assenting vote

platonic

see Appendix 1

pm

see **post meridiem**

politikon zoon *(Gk)*

(pol-IT-i-kon ZOH-on) (man is by nature) a political animal (Aristotle)

pons asinorum *(Lat)*

(PONS as-in-OR-um) lit: the ass's bridge; problem inaccessible to people of limited wit

post hoc ergo propter hoc *(Lat)*	*(post hok erg-oh PROP-ter hok) lit:* after this, therefore because of this; the fallacy that temporal succession implies causal relationship
post meridiem *(Lat)*	*(post mer-ID-i-em)* after noon *(abbr:* **pm)**
post mortem *(Lat)*	*(post MOR-tem) lit:* after death; usually applied to examination of a corpse to discover the cause of death
post scriptum *(Lat)*	*(post SCRIP-tum)* addition to a letter added after signature (*abbr:* **PS)**
pp	*see* **per procurationem**
priapism	*see* Appendix 1
prima facie *(Lat)*	*(PREE-ma FAK-i-e)* at first glance, on first sight; **prima facie** case: one in which initial evidence is thought sufficient to justify further examination and prosecution
primus inter pares *(Lat)*	*(PREE-mus in-ter PAH-rays)* first among equals; spokesman of a group which is not differentiated by rank
pro et con(tra) *(Lat)*	*(PROH et CON-tra)* for and against (an argument, position, motion, etc)
pro forma *(Lat)*	*(proh FOR-ma)* as a formality; **pro forma** invoice: one issued in advance of the despatch of goods
pro rata *(Lat)*	*(proh RAH-ta)* in proportion, as a given ratio of
protean	*see* Appendix 1
pro tem	*see* **pro tempore**
pro tempore *(Lat)*	*(proh TEM-po-RAY)* temporarily, for the moment *(abbr:* **pro tem)**
proxime accessit *(Lat)*	*(PROX-i-may ak-KES-sit)* runner-up, second-best
PS	*see* **post scriptum**

pyrrhic   *see* Appendix 1

Q

QED   *see* **quod erat demonstrandum**

QEF   *see* **quod erat faciendum**

qua *(Lat)*   *(kwah)* as, in the capacity of, considered as

quaesitum *(Lat)*   *(KWAI-see-tum) lit:* (something) which is sought after; that which is to be determined, the answer or solution

quantum libet *(Lat)*   *(KWAN-tum LI-bet)* as much as you please, sufficient amount

quantum meruit *(Lat)*   *(KWAN-tum ME-ru-it) lit:* as much as was deserved; (in law) fair recompense

quantum sufficit *(Lat)*   *(KWAN-tum suf-FIK-it)* as much as is necessary, sufficient amount

quantum vis *(Lat)*   *(KWAN-tum WEES)* as much as you will, as much as you wish

quid pro quo *(Lat)*   *(kwid proh kwoh) lit:* something for something; compensation for a concession, etc; (something given) in return for a service rendered

quis custodiet ipsos custodes *(Lat)*   *(kwis kus-TOH-di-et IP-sos kus-TOH-days)* who is to control the authorities?

quod erat demonstrandum *(Lat)*   *(kwod e-rat DAY-mons-TRAN-dum)* that which was to be proved *(abbr:* **QED**)

quod erat faciendum *(Lat)*   *(kwod e-rat FAK-i-END-um)* that which was to be carried out *(abbr:* **QEF**)

quod vide *(Lat)*   *(kwod WEE-de)* for which see, refer to (used in cross references) *(abbr:* **qv**)

quo jure *(Lat)*   *(kwoh yoo-re)* by what right, on what authority (do you act)?

quondam *(Lat)*   *(KWOHN-dam)* former, once

quot homines, tot sententiae *(Lat)*	*(kwot HOM-in-es tot sen-TENT-i-ah)* there are as many opinions as there are men (Erasmus)
quo vadis *(Lat)*	*(kwo WAH-dis)* where are you going? where are you heading?
qv	*see* **quod vide**

R

radix malorum *(Lat)*	*(RAH-dix ma-LOR-um)* the root of all evil; often used in reference to greed or avarice and sometimes to stupidity
radix malorum est cupiditas *(Lat)*	*(RAH-dix ma-LOR-um est ku-PID-i-tas)* money is the root of all evil
rara avis *(Lat)*	*(RAH-ra A-vis) lit:* rare bird; something rarely encountered
ratio decidendi *(Lat)*	*(RA-ti-oh day-kid-END-ee)* method of decision-making; the essentials of a judgement, the reasons for a particular decision (*cf* **obiter dictum**)
rebus sic stantibus *(Lat)*	*(RAY-bus seek STAN-i-bus)* things being the way they are; (in law) in these particular circumstances
recto *(Lat)*	*(REK-toh)* the right-hand page of a book (*opp:* **verso**)
reductio ad absurdum *(Lat)*	*(re-DUK-ti-oh ad ab-SURD-um)* method of disproving a proposition by assuming a conclusion to be incorrect and working back to find a contradiction
requiescat in pace *(Lat)*	*(re-kwi-es-KAT in PAH-ke)* may he rest in peace (*abbr:* **RIP**)
res gestae *(Lat)*	*(res GEST-ai)* material facts, matters relevant to a legal case
res ipsa loquitur *(Lat)*	*(res IP-sa LOK-wi-tur) lit:* the thing in itself speaks; it is all rather obvious; the situation speaks for itself

res judicata *(Lat)*	*(res YOO-dic-AH-ta) lit:* thing which has been judged; closed case, matter which has been settled
res nihili *(Lat)*	*(res NI-hil-ee)* thing of no consequence, trifling matter
rhadamantine	*see* Appendix 1
rigor mortis *(Lat)*	*(RIG-or MOR-tis)* the stiffness of a corpse, developing within hours of death
RIP	*see* **requiescat in pace**

S

salus populi suprema lex est *(Lat)*	*(SA-lus POP-oo-li sup-RAY-ma lex est)* the safety of the people is the supreme law; utilitarian belief that the only standard by which government can be measured is its impact on the material welfare of the governed
sapphism	*see* Appendix 1
saturnalia	*see* Appendix 1
saturnine	*see* Appendix 1
satyr	*see* Appendix 1
sc	*see* **sculpsit**
scepsis *(Gk)*	*(SKEP-sis) lit:* inquiry, philosophic doubt, sceptical philosophy
sculp	*see* **sculpsit**
sculpsit *(Lat)*	*(SKULP-sit) lit:* he engraved (it); engraver's signature on engraving (*abbr:* **sc, sculp**)
Scylla and Charybdis	*see* Appendix 1
secundum ordinem *(Lat)*	*(sec-UND-um OR-di-nem) lit:* according to sequence; in order, arranged sequentially

semper fidelis *(Lat)* — *(SEM-per fi-DAY-lis)* ever faithful, loyal throughout

sensu stricto *(Lat)* — *(SEN-soo STRIK-too)* strictly speaking

sibyl — *see* Appendix 1

sic *(Lat)* — *(seek) lit:* so, thus, as it was, in this way; inserted parenthetically into a text to indicate the occurrence of an anomaly or misspelling which has not been corrected for the purpose of quotation

sic passim *(Lat)* — *(seek PAS-sim) lit:* thus throughout; inserted in a text to indicate an anomaly or misspelling which occurs throughout a text and is not altered by the author quoting it

sic transit gloria mundi *(Lat)* — *(seek TRAN-sit GLOR-i-a MUND-ee)* thus passes the glory of the world, thus fades worldly splendour

silent leges inter arma *(Lat)* — *(SIL-ent LEG-es IN-ter AR-ma)* war silences the law

simpliciter *(Lat)* — *(sim-PLIK-i-ter)* wholly and absolutely; in every respect

sine mora *(Lat)* — *(si-ne MOHR-ah)* without delay

sine qua non *(Lat)* — *(si-ne kwah NON)* precondition (*see* **causa sine qua non**)

siren — *see* Appendix 1

si vis pacem para bellum *(Lat)* — *(see wees PAH-kem PAR-a BEL-lum)* if you want peace, prepare for war

socratic — *see* Appendix 1

solitudinem faciunt pacem appellant *(Lat)* — *(SOL-i-TOO-din-em FAK-i-unt PAH-kem AP-pel-lant)* they create a desert and call it a peace; Calcugas, chief of the Caledonians, on Roman imperialism

spartan — *see* Appendix 1

speude bradeos
(Gr)
(SPEUD-e BRAD-e-ohs) lit: hasten slowly; more haste, less speed; translated into Latin as **festina lente,** the dictum of the Emperor Augustus

splendide mendax
(Lat)
(SPLEN-did-e MEN-dax) splendidly false; Horace describing Cleopatra, the enemy of Rome

sponte sua *(Lat)*
(SPON-tay SU-ah) of one's own free will

stasis *(Gk)*
(STA-sis) cessation in the flow of blood, blockage in any situation

status quo *(Lat)*
(STA-tus kwoh) things as they are; the existing state of things

status quo ante
(Lat)
(STA-tus kwoh AN-tay) situation prevailing before (a period of conflict, etc)

stoic
see Appendix 1

stupor mundi *(Lat)*
(STU-por MUND-ee) wonder of the world

stygian
see Appendix 1

sub judice *(Lat)*
(sub YOO-di-cay) lit: under a judge; under judgement, not yet decided; (in law) under judicial consideration (and therefore not to be disclosed to the public)

sub poena *(Lat)*
(sub PEEN-ah) lit: under a penalty; writ demanding, on penalty, that one attend court; usually subpoena in English

sub rosa *(Lat)*
(sub ROH-sah) lit: under the rose (a mark of secrecy); secret, in confidence, under pledge of secrecy

sub voce *(Lat)*
(sub WOH-kay) under that heading, under that category

suggestio falsi
(Lat)
(sug-GEST-ioh FAL-see) misrepresentation to conceal truth;

suppression of the truth that is not quite a lie (*cf* **suppressio veri**)

sui generis *(Lat)*   *(SU-ee GEN-er-is)* unique, in a class by itself, peculiar

sui juris *(Lat)*   *(SU-ee YOOR-is)* (of an age) capable of assuming full responsibility and exercising judgement

summa *(Lat)*   *(SUM-ma)* summary treatise ranging over the whole subject

suppressio veri *(Lat)*   *(sup-PRESS-i-oh WER-i) lit:* suppression of truth; wilful misrepresentation

sybaritic   *see* Appendix 1

T

taedium vitae *(Lat)*   *(TAI-di-um WEE-tai)* weariness with life

tantalus   *see* Appendix 1

tempus edax rerum *(Lat)*   *(TEM-pus ED-ax RER-um) lit:* time consumes all things; everything is transitory (Ovid)

tempus fugit *(Lat)*   *(TEM-pus FUG-it)* time passes quickly (*see* **hora fugit**)

terminus ad quem *(Lat)*   *(TER-min-us ad kwem)* the point towards which action tends; the latest possible date for an event or process

terminus a quo *(Lat)*   *(TER-min-us ah kwo)* starting point; the earliest possible date for an event or process

terpsichorean   *see* Appendix 1

terra incognita *(Lat)*   *(TER-ra in-COG-nit-a)* unknown realm or territory, unexplored region (geographical, scientific, philosophical, etc)

thalatta thalatta *(Gk)* — *(thal-AT-ta thal-AT-ta)* the sea, the sea; the exulting cry of Xenophon's men on seeing the sea

themis — *see* Appendix 1

thespian — *see* Appendix 1

titan — *see* Appendix 1

trojan — *see* Appendix 1

trojan horse — *see* Appendix 1

tu quoque *(Lat)* — *(too KWO-kwe) lit:* and you also; riposte to signify that an accusation may be turned against the accuser

typhoon — *see* Appendix 1

U

ultima ratio regum *(Lat)* — *(UL-ti-ma RA-ti-oh REG-um)* the final argument (of kings), ie force

ultima thule *(Lat)* — *(UL-ti-mah TOO-lay)* the furthest point accessible

ultra vires *(Lat)* — *(UL-tra WI-res)* outside one's jurisdiction, beyond the scope of one's power or authority (*opp:* **intra vires**)

urbi et orbi *(Lat)* — *(UR-bi et OR-bi)* to the city (of Rome) and to the world; papal blessing or pronouncement

ut infra *(Lat)* — *(ut IN-fra)* (direction to) see below (in a text)

ut supra *(Lat)* — *(ut-SUP-ra)* (direction to) see above (in a text)

V

vade mecum *(Lat)* — *(WAH-day MAY-cum) lit:* come with me; guidebook, ready-reference text (designed to be carried about)

variae lectiones	*see* **varia lectio**
varia lectio *(Lat)*	*(WAH-ri-a LEK-ti-oh)* variant reading (plu: **varia lectiones**)
variatim *(Lat)*	*(WAH-ri-AH-tim)* variously, in various ways
variorum	*see* **cum notis variorum**
veni, vidi, vici *(Lat)*	*(WAY-ni WEE-di WEE-ki)* I came, I saw, I conquered; statement attributed to Caesar after his victory over Pharnaces, an Asian king
verbatim (et literatim) *(Lat)*	*(wer-BAY-tim et lit-er-AH-tim)* word for word (and letter for letter); as it was written, quoted exactly
verso *(Lat)*	*(WER-so)* the left-hand page of a book; the reverse side of a sheet (*opp:* **recto**)
vestigia *(Lat)*	*(WEST-i-gee-ah) lit:* footprints; traces, remains
via media *(Lat)*	*(WEE-a MED-i-a)* middle course between two extremes
vice versa *(Lat)*	*(WEE-ke WER-sah) lit:* positions between reversed; conversely, the other way around
videlicet *(Lat)*	*(WEE-de-LIK-et) lit:* one may see; namely, that is to say; usually follows a passage needing explanation (*abbr:* **viz**)
vi et armis *(Lat)*	*(WEE et AR-mees)* by force of arms
vinculum matrimoniie *(Lat)*	*(WIN-cu-lum MAT-ri-MOH-ni-i)* the ties of marriage
viva voce *(Lat)*	*(WEE-wa WO-ke)* oral examination
vive ut vivas *(Lat)*	*(WEE-we ut WEE-was)* live that you may live (hereafter)
viz	*see* **videlicet**

volenti non fit injuria *(Lat)*   *(wo-LEN-tee non fit in-YOO-ri-a)* there can be no injury to he who consents

vox audita perit litera scripta manet *(Lat)*   *(wox OWD-i-ta PER-it LIT-er-a SCRIP-ta MAN-et)* the voice, once heard, perishes but the written word remains

vox populi *(Lat)*   *(wox POP-u-li) lit:* the voice of the people; the general verdict, public opinion

vox populi, vox dei *(Lat)*   *(WOX POP-u-lee WOX DE-ee) lit:* the voice of the people is the voice of God; the voice of the people is supreme

Z

zephyr   *see* Appendix 1

French

French has had a considerable influence on the evolution of English and is the source of many borrowed terms and phrases. Many, such as 'restaurant' and 'café', have been wholly absorbed and are not included in this section. But others, particularly terms in literature, ballet and the arts in general, have only been partly absorbed and are not always accurately defined or generally known.

Pronunciation

The English syllabic equivalent given in brackets after each entry is intended only as a guide. In French, there are several sounds which cannot be accurately represented in English, and the rules outlined below should be noted.

c	may be soft, like the English *s*, or hard and the text should be followed
d	silent at the end of a word
e	may be open, as the *air* in f*air*, or closed, as the *e* in n*e*ck
é	pronounced as the *ay* in d*ay*
g	may be hard or soft and the text should be followed
h	usually silent
i	as the *i* in mach*i*ne
j	soft, as the *z* in a*z*ure
n	almost silent at the end of a word
r	usually emphasized
s	silent at the end of a word, though it may be pronounced if the next word begins with a vowel
t	silent at the end of a word
u	similar to *oo* in English but shorter
y	usually pronounced as the *ee* in n*ee*d

A

à bas	*(ah BAH)* down with!
à bientôt	*(ah BYEN-toh) lit:* soon; *fig:* see you later!
abondance	*(ah-bonn-DAHNSE)* (in whist) the attempt to win nine tricks
abondance déclarée	*(ah-bonn-DAHNSE day-clah-RAY)* (in whist) the attempt to win all the tricks; also used generally to indicate ambition
à bon droit	*(ah bonn DRWA) lit:* with good reason; with justice
à bras ouverts	*(ah BRAHS oo-ver) lit:* with open arms, cordially (receiving guests, etc)
accueil	*(ah-KWEE)* greeting, welcome, reception
acharnement	*(ah-SHAR-ne-mon)* relentlessness, ferocity, extreme determination
acharnement au travail	*(ah-SHAR-ne-mon oh trah-VYE)* addiction to work
à cheval	*(ah she-VAHL)* on horseback; used in roulette to indicate a bet placed across two adjacent numbers
à compte	*(ah COM-te)* part payment, instalment
à contrecoeur	*(ah CON-tre-KUHR)* grudgingly, against one's wishes or inclination

à corps perdu	*(ah COR per-DOO) lit:* until the loss of the body; desperately, recklessly
acte gratuit	*(AKT grat-WEE)* impulsive act; act with no ostensible cause
actionnaire	*(AK-syo-nair)* shareholder, stockholder
(les) actualités	*(lehz ac-too-al-ee-TAY)* current events, news
ADC	*see* **aide de camp**
à demi	*(ah de-MEE)* 'half' done, badly done, incomplete
à dessein	*(ah dess-AN) lit:* by design; on purpose, intentionally
à deux	*(ah DER)* for two people, between two people (usually used in the sense of for only two)
adieu	*(ad-YUH)* goodbye; derived from *à Dieu* and suggesting finality
affaire d'amour	*(ah-FAIR da-MUHR) lit:* matter of love; love affair
affaire de coeur	*(ah-FAIR de KUHR)* matter of the heart; love affair
affaire d'honneur	*(ah-FAIR don-UHR)* matter of principle, duel (often used ironically in English)
affaire d'intérêt	*(ah-FAIR dan-te-REH)* matter involving self-interest; matter of money
affolé	*(ah-fol-LAY)* driven to madness, distracted (often used with reference to love, anger, etc)
agent provocateur	*(AH-jon pro-voc-ah-TUHR) lit:* agent of provocation; one who is commissioned to incite others to criminal acts; one such planted in a crowd to fuel a disturbance or riot

agiotage   *(ah-jyo-TAJ)* stock-jobbing, illicit speculation

agréments (de la vie)   *(ah-grey-MON)* refinements (of life), embellishments, amenities, adornments

à haute voix   *(ah oat VWAH)* at the top of one's voice

aide de camp   *(ED de com)* trusted assistant, confidential adviser to a senior officer (*abbr:* **ADC**)

aide-mémoire   *(ED-may-mwar) lit:* aid to memory; memorandum (often used in diplomacy); book acting as an aid to memory

aigreur   *(ay-GRUHR)* acrimony, acerbity, sourness, harshness

ainé   *(ay-NAY)* the elder, eldest

à la   *(ah lah)* in the manner of, following the style of

à la bourgeoise   *(ah lah BOOR-jwa)* in the style of the middle classes, conventionally

à la broche   *(ah lah BROSH) lit:* on the spit; cooked on a skewer, barbecued

à la carte   *(ah lah KAHRT) lit:* on the card, according to the menu; with each item priced separately (*cf* **table d'hôte**)

à la française   *(ah lah fron-SAIS)* in the French style

à la grecque   *(ah lah GRECK)* in the Greek style

à la lanterne   *(ah lah LONG-tern) lit:* to the lamp-post! lynch him!; slogan derived from the French revolution in which mobs hanged aristocrats and others from the supports of street lights

à la mode   *(ah lah mohd)* in fashion

à l'anglaise   *(ah long-GLEHS)* in the English style

à la page   *(ah lah pahj)* up to date, in line with the latest fashions

à la parisienne   *(ah lah pah-ri-ZI-ENN)* in the Parisian style

à la russe   *(ah lah ROOS)* in the Russian style

à l'improviste   *(ah lahm-pro-VEEST)* suddenly, unawares

ambiance   *(am-bie-ons)* surroundings, atmosphere, the prevailing spirit

âme de boue   *(AHM de BOO) lit:* soul of mud; base soul, ungenerous spirit

âme perdue   *(AHM per-DOO) lit:* lost soul; desperate individual

à merveille   *(ah mer-VAY)* marvellously, wonderfully

ami de cour   *(ah-mee de coor)* false friend; *colloq:* fairweather friend

à moitié   *(ah mwat-EE-AY)* half, part, by halves

amour propre   *(ah-MOOR PROH-PR)* vanity, desire for admiration, self esteem

ancien régime   *(AHN-see-en RAY-JEEM)* the old order; used to describe France before the revolution of 1789, or more generally with reference to any established system which has been supplanted

animateur   *(an-ee-mah-TUHR)* one who is capable of simplifying difficult concepts for the benefit of a general audience

appellation contrôlée   *(app-ell-A-see-yon con-trol-AY) lit:* registered trade name; guarantee on a bottle of French wine both of its place of origin and of the standard of quality traditionally associated with that place

apéritif   *(ah-peh-ree-TEEF) lit:* appetizer; drink taken before a meal

après nous le déluge — *(ah-preh NOO le day-LOOJ) lit:* after us the deluge; a premonition of impending political and social collapse attributed to Madame de Pompadour, the mistress of Louis XV

à propos — *(ah pro-POH)* pertinent to, with reference to, relevant

arrière-pensée — *(ahr-ree-EHR-pon-SAY) lit:* behind thought; mental reservation; ulterior motive

arriviste — *(ah-ree-VEEST)* social climber, person with money who lacks the veneer of ancient gentility

arrondissement — *(arr-on-DEES-mon)* area, district, administrative division of French **département**

art brut — *(ar broo) lit:* raw art; the art of the untrained; the notion that all representations, including graffiti, children's scribblings, etc are art

art nouveau — *(ar noo-VOH)* architectural style characterized by ornamental design and decoration which developed at the end of the nineteenth century

art sacré — *(ar SAK-ray) lit:* sacred art; twentieth-century movement which sought to re-establish religious art in the face of the supposed threat of modern and abstract art

atelier — *(ah-tell-YAY)* workshop, studio (usually of artist)

à tout prix — *(ah too PREE)* at all costs, at any price

attaché — *(ah-tah-SHAY)* senior official of an embassy

au courant — *(oh COO-ron)* up to date, well-informed

au-dessus de la mêlée — *(oh-de-SOO de la MEH-lay) lit:* above the struggle; expression of detachment from and indifference to the 1914-18 war (the term was introduced by an article in the *Journal de Genève* in 1914)

au fait   *(oh FAY) lit:* well-versed, expert

au fond   *(oh fon)* at root, fundamentally

au pair   *(oh pear) lit:* at par; usually refers to a young servant/home help (usually foreign) prepared to work in return for free board

au premier coup   *(oh pre-MYER COO) lit:* at the first blow; completion of a painting at a single attempt, in one session

au premier coup d'oeil   *(oh pre-MYER COO doy)* at first glance, at first sight

au prix coûtant   *(oh prie koo-TON)* at cost price

au revoir   *(oh re-VWAR)* goodbye (until we meet again)

auteur   *(oh-TUHR) lit:* author, creator; notion of film director as 'author' which became current in the 1950s; the true **auteur** was responsible for the whole conception of a film, not merely its realization on the screen

autrefois acquit   *(oh-tre-FWA ah-KEE)* (in law) previously acquitted of a charge and therefore not liable to judgement for the offence

autre temps, autre moeurs   *(OH-tre-TOM OH-tre MUHR) lit:* other times, other ways; values change with the times

avant garde   *(ah-VON GAHR)* ahead of one's time, in the forefront (often used of artistic or literary trends)

à votre santé   *(ah VOT-re son-TAY)* to your health! cheers!

B

baccalauréat *(bah-kah-loh-reh-AH)* bachelorship (of arts, science, etc) taken at the end of pre-university studies in France; school-leaving examination; qualification conferred on successful candidates

bagatelle *(bag-ah-TELL)* trifle, bauble, trinket

ballon d'essai *(bal-LON des-SAY) lit:* trial balloon; tentative approach, prototype, initial attempt

battre le pavé *(BAT-re le pah-VAY) lit:* to thump the pavement; to loaf around, to idle

beau geste *(boh ZHEST)* grand gesture

beau monde *(boh MOHN-de) lit:* beautiful world; fashionable society

beaux arts *(boh ZAR)* fine arts

beaux esprits *see* **bel esprit**

beaux yeux *(boh ZYER) lit:* beautiful eyes; good looks

bel air *(bel EHR)* grace, poise, good deportment

belle époque *(BELL ay-POCK) lit:* beautiful era; the period 1900-14

bel esprit *(BELL es-PREE)* great wit; *plu:* **beaux esprits**

belle mort *(BEL more)* natural death

belles lettres *(bell LET-rah)* serious literature: essays, criticism, aesthetics, 'quality' fiction and poetry

bête noire *(bett nwah) lit:* black beast; pet aversion, something provoking fear and trepidation

bêtise *(bet-EEZ)* ignorance, stupidity

bien être	*(byen etr)* well-being
bijou	*(bee-ZEW) lit:* jewel; exquisite miniature
billet doux	*(bi-yay doo) lit:* sweet note; love letter
blague	*(blahg)* humbug, joke
blagueur	*(blahg-UHR)* one who indulges in jokes
blasé	*(blah-ZAY)* world-weary, tired of pleasure
boiserie	*(BWA-zer-EE)* panelling, usually decorated with elaborate hand carvings
bombé	*(bom-BAY) lit:* bomb-shaped; bulging; curved; used especially with reference to furniture
bon appétit	*(bon AP-eh-tee)* (have a) good appetite; *fig:* enjoy your meal
bon compagnon	*(bon com-pan-NJON)* good companion
bon diable	*(bon dee-AHBL)* good-humoured man
bondieuserie	*(bon-dews-er-EE)* over-sentimental religious art
bon goût	*(bon GOO)* good taste
bonhomie	*(bon-OM-EE)* good-heartedness, good nature
bonhomme	*(bon-OM)* good, simple, straightforward man
bon marché	*(bon mahr-SHAY)* cheap, inexpensive; a bargain
bon mot	*(bon moh)* witty comment, aphorism, memorable remark
bonne foi	*(bonn FWA)* good faith
bon ton	*(bon ton)* good style, polished manner
bon vivant	*(bon vee-VANT) lit:* good living; one who savours the good things of life

bon viveur	*(bon vee-VUHR) lit:* good liver; one who lives luxuriously
bon voyage	*(bon voy-AHJ)* (have a) good journey
bouffant	*(bou-FAHN)* puffed up (usually used to describe such a hairstyle)
bourgeois	*(boor-JWA) lit:* city dweller; (member of the) middle class; person with conventional ideas
Bourse	*(boor-se) lit:* purse; the French stock exchange
bric-à-brac	*(brick-ah-brack)* miscellaneous old trinkets, ornaments, etc
brise-soleil	*(breeze-soh-lay) lit:* sun-break; arrangement of slats used to shade window openings
brouhaha	*(BREW-ha-ha)* hubbub, commotion
bruitisme	*(BRWEE-teesm)* Futurist notion that all noise constitutes art

C

cachet	*(ca-SHAY)* seal conferring authority; kudos, credit
cadre	*(cad-re) lit:* frame, framework; permanent nucleus, establishment; (member of) communist unit
ça ira	*(sah eer-AH)* it will be all right (French revolutionary song)
caisson	*(KES-on) lit:* chest; watertight chamber used in laying foundations in water or marshland
camaraderie	*(kahm-ah-RAHD-er-EE)* good fellowship
canaille	*(KAHN-ay)* the common people, the rabble
canard	*(kahn-AR) lit:* duck; rumour, hoax

ça ne fait rien	*(sah ne FAY ree-yen)* it does not matter, it is not important
carte blanche	*(kart BLAHNSH)* complete freedom, authority to act at will
carte de visite	*(kart de viz-EET)* calling card, visiting card
cartel	*(kar-tell)* group of companies with common interests
cartouche	*(kar-TOOSH)* decorative scroll or frame; (in architecture) piece of applied decoration on a wall in similar form
cause célèbre	*(kose say-LEH-bre) lit:* celebrated case; issue provoking considerable public interest; particularly notorious lawsuit
celui qui veut, peut	*(se-LWEE kee VUHR PUHR)* he who will, can; *colloq:* where there's a will, there's a way
cercle privé	*(SER-cla pree-VAY) lit:* private group; private gaming party
c'est à dire	*(seht ah DEER)* that is to say; in other words
c'est autre chose	*(seht awt-re SHOSE) lit:* that is another thing; that is different
c'est la guerre	*(seh lah GERR)* they are the conventions of war (expression of resignation)
c'est la vie	*(seh lah vee)* oh well! that's life! (expression of resignation)
c'est magnifique mais ce n'est pas la guerre	*(seh mah-NYEE-FEEK meh se neh pah la GERR)* it is splendid but it is not war; reference by the French Marshal Bosquet to the glorious self-destruction of the British cavalry in the charge of the Light Brigade at the battle of Balaclava in 1854
c'est selon	*(seh se-lon)* that depends (on circumstances, etc)

c'est tout dire   *(seh too-DEER)* (you have said) all there
is to say

chacun son goût   *(shac-un son GOO) lit:* everyone to his
own taste; tastes differ

chagrin   *(shag-ran)* mortification, vexation

chagrin d'amour   *(shag-ran dah-MOOR)* affliction of love,
distress bred of unhappiness in love

chaise longue   *(shez lohng) lit:* long chair; sofa with a
single back rest

chanteuse   *(shan-tuhz)* female (café) singer

chapeau rouge   *(sha-po ROOJ) lit:* red hat; cardinal's hat
(and thus its wearer)

charabanc   *see* **char à bancs**

char à bancs   *(shar a bong) lit:* seated carriage; bus,
coach (for sightseeing, day trips, etc)

charcuterie   *(shar-KOO-terr-ee) lit:* pork butcher's
trade; shop where cooked meats
(especially pork) are sold

château   *(shah-TOH)* castle (the name of which is
often applied to the locally produced
wine)

châteaux en   *(shah-TOH on esp-ANG-nh) lit:* castles in
Espagne   Spain; castles in the air

chef d'oeuvre   *(SHAY duhvr) lit:* main (piece of) work;
masterpiece, major work (of art)

chemin de fer   *see* **Métro**
Métropolitain

cherchez la femme   *(sher-shay la fam) lit:* look for the
woman (as the probable explanation of
disaster, tragedy, etc)

chevaux de frise   *(she-VOH de FREEZ) lit:* Frisian horses;
portable barrier of interconnected
wooden poles with metal tips used to halt
advancing cavalry; the defence was

developed in the seventeenth century by the Frisians who had no cavalry forces

chez *(shay)* at the house or place of; with, among

chez la famille *(shay la fam-EEYE)* at the family's home, with the family

chez moi *(shay MWA)* at my home

chien méchant *(shee-an may-shon) lit:* naughty dog; beware of dog

chinoiserie *(shin-nwa-ser-EE)* European imitations of Chinese decorative and architectural forms (usually eighteenth century)

cinéaste *(seen-ay-ast)* devotee of the cinema

cinéma vérité *(see-nay-MAH vay-ree-TAY) lit:* cinema of truth; style of film-making that emphasizes realism

claqueur *(klah-CUHR)* someone paid to applaud at a performance

clique *(kleek)* coterie, exclusive group

collage *(kol-AHJ)* abstract work of art created by pasting together various materials, shapes, etc

comédie noire *(com-AY-dee NWAR) lit:* black comedy; comedy based on tragic or desperate circumstances; associated with the French playwright Jean Anouilh who wrote a series of **pièces noires** in the 1930s and 1940s, and developed by Samuel Beckett

comme ci, comme ça *(com-SEE com-SAH)* you win some, you lose some; so-so

comme il faut *(kom eel foh) lit:* as is necessary; proper (behaviour, etc), socially acceptable (usually used ironically or sarcastically in English)

compère *(COM-pair)* announcer at a revue or

	other entertainment; accomplice in crime, prank, etc
concierge	*(con-see-ERJ)* porter, janitor, doorkeeper
congé	*(con-JAY)* leave, permission to depart
connoisseur	*(conn-oh-SUHR) lit:* one who has knowledge; expert in a given field (arts, antiques, food, wine, etc)
conservatoire	*(con-ser-VA-TWAR)* conservatory, school of music, art, etc
contretemps	*(CON-truh-tom) lit:* against time; mishap, unfortunate event, inconvenience
coquette	*(ko-KET)* habitual flirt
cordon bleu	*(kor-don BLUH) lit:* blue ribbon (of the Order of the Garter); first-class cook or cookery
cordon sanitaire	*(COR-don SAN-ee-TEHR)* cordoning off an infected area; also applied to the isolation of a politically sensitive area or subject
corps	*(kor)* body or group of individuals (as in Marine **corps,** etc)
corps de ballet	*(kor de bah-lay)* those in ballet troupe who do not dance solo parts
corps diplomatique	*(kor dip-loh-mah-TEEK) lit:* diplomatic body; foreign office
coterie	*(co-ter-EE)* clique, closed group
couchette	*(coo-SHET) lit:* sleeper; sleeping berth on train; railway carriage with sleeping berths
coup	*see* **coup d'état**
coup d'autorité	*(COO doh-tor-ee-tay) lit:* blow of authority; act of authority

coup d'éclat	*(COO day-KLAH)* brilliant manoeuvre, dashing stroke
coup de foudre	*(COO de FOO-dra) lit:* flash of lightning, thunderbolt; sudden passion, shock or stroke
coup de grâce	*(COO de GRAHSS) lit:* grace stroke; final blow, finishing stroke
coup de main	*(COO de MAHN)* surprise attack, unexpected blow
coup d'état	*(COO day-TAH)* violent or unconstitutional change of government (often abbreviated to **coup** in English)
coup de théâtre	*(COO de tay-AHT-ra)* dramatically sudden act, sensational occurrence, stage trick performed for effect
crèche	*(kresh)* day nursery, nursery for the children of working mothers
crème de la crème	*(KREM de la KREM) lit:* cream of the cream; the ultimate, the top level (usually used to denote 'the best people', highest society)
cri de coeur	*(CREE de KUHR)*cry from the heart, heartfelt plea
cri de la conscience	*(CREE de la kon-see-yons)* voice of conscience
croix de guerre	*(krwa de GERR) lit:* cross of war; medal
cul de sac	*(kool de sack) lit:* bottom of a sack, street or pathway closed at one end, street with no through road
cy près	*(SEE-pray)* (in law) the attempt to execute a person's wishes as closely as possible when the instructions (eg of a will) cannot be followed exactly

D

dame de compagnie *(DAM de com-pan-gnie)* lady's maid or companion

dame d'honneur *(DAM don-UHR)* maid of honour

danse macabre *(DAHNSE mah-CAH-br)* dance of death (usually applied to music)

débâcle *(day-BAH-cl)* collapse, complete breakdown, fiasco

début *(day-BOO)* first performance, initial appearance (in society, on stage, in sport)

débutante *(day-BOO-TANT)* person making a first appearance, performance, etc

déclassé *(day-clas-say) lit:* declassed; displaced from one's former social station, of reduced status

déclassement *(day-CLASS-mon)* loss of social position, fall from one class to a lower class

décollage *(day-COL-AJ)* art form achieved by tearing strips from a collage

décolletage *(DAY-col-let-TAJ)* low cut of a dress, the revealing of the neck and shoulders

dégagé *(DAY-gah-JAY)* free, informal, unaligned, uncommitted, unconstrained

d'égal à égal *(deg-al ah eg-AL) lit:* equal to equal; equally, on equal terms; man to man

dégoût *(day-GOO)* distaste, disgust

de haut en bas *(de OAT on BAH) lit:* from above to below; contemptuously, superciliously

déjà vu *(DAY-jah voo)* (the experience of) seeming to have previously encountered a thing, event, or place

de mal en pis	*(de mal on PEE)* from bad to worse
démarche	*(DAY-marsh)* step, manoeuvre, course of action (usually employed to indicate a new direction or change of policy)
demi mondaine	*(DEM-ee MOHND-en)* woman who lives on the fringe of society, woman of doubtful repute, inhabitant of the **demi monde**
demi monde	*(DEM-ee MOHND) lit:* half-world; class peripheral to society, those of questionable reputation
démodé	*(DAY-mo-DAY)* out of fashion, old-fashioned
dénouement	*(DAY-new-MON) lit:* unravelling (of plot); result, upshot, resolution, outcome (usually of a play, novel, etc)
de nouveau	*(de noo-VO)* anew, afresh
de par le roi	*(de par le RWA)* in the name of the king
département	*(DAY-par-ta-MON)* department; province, largest administrative unit in France
dépaysé	*(day-PAY-zay)* removed from one's country; adrift from one's natural environment
de pis en pis	*(de peace son pee)* from bad to worse
de plein gré	*(de plen GRAY)* freely, willingly, voluntarily
déprimé	*(DAY-pree-may)* depressed, down-hearted, low-spirited, discouraged
déraciné	*(DAY-ras-see-NAY) lit:* uprooted; removed from (one's) natural environment
dérangé	*(DAY-ron-JAY)* out of order, in confusion (things); mad (person)

de rigueur	*(de ree-GUHR)* strictly necessary, compulsory; required by the rules of etiquette
dernier cri	*(DAIR-nee-ay CREE)* lit: the last word; the very latest, in fashion
désagrément	*(DAY-zag-ray-MON)* embarrassment, unpleasantness
déshabillé	*(DAYS-ab-ee-yay)* lit: undressed; in a state of sloppiness, undress, etc
désolé	*(day-ZOH-lay)* desolate, disconsolate, heart-broken
détente	*(day-TONT)* relaxation, especially reduction of tension or animosity between nations
de trop	*(de TROH)* in excess, superfluous (things); unwanted presence (person); (often used with a suggestion of vulgarity)
dirigisme	*(dee-ree-jeesm)* lit: direction, control; policy of state intervention in economic and social affairs (cf **laisser faire/laissez faire**)
dirigiste	*(dee-ree-jeest)* lit: directed, controlled; adjectival use of **dirigisme**
diseur/diseuse	*(dee-ZUHR/dee-ZUHZ)* performer (male or female) delivering monologues
divertissement	*(dee-vair-TEES-mon)* small-scale work (often as a foil or counter to a major presentation)
double entendre	*(doub-luh on-TON-druh)* ambiguous expression, phrase with two meanings; often a deliberate and **risqué** ambiguity
du meilleur rang	*(doo MAY-yuhr RAHNG)* lit: of the best rank; of the highest order, aristocratic
d'un certain âge	*(duhn SEHR-tan AHJ)* middle aged;

polite term, as in a woman **d'un certain âge**

E

ébauche	*(ay-BOHSH)* sketch, rough draft, model (for work of art, etc)
échelon	*(AY-shel-lon)* rung of a ladder, level within a hierarchy; (occasionally anglicized in pronunciation as *ESH-el-on*)
éclat	*(AY-clah)* brilliance, success
écrasez l'infâme	*(ay-KRAZ-ay lahn-FAHM)* crush the filthy object, root out the infamy (used by Voltaire, with reference to the Catholic Church)
élan	*(ay-LON)* flair, dashing quality
élan vital	*(ay-LON VEE-tal) lit:* vital impetus; life force, source of an individual's motivations; the notion of the life force is important in the philosophy of Schopenhauer and Henri Bergson
élite	*(ay-LEET)* upper stratum in society; group with certain privileges
embarras de richesses	*(om-BA-RA de ree-SHESS) lit:* embarrassment of riches; abundance of wealth, goods, etc
embarras du choix	*(om-BA-RA doo-SHWA) lit:* embarrassment of choice; state of not knowing which of many equally promising alternatives to choose
émeute	*(ay-moat)* popular rising, insurrection, riot, tumult
émigré	*(ay-mee-gray)* exile, refugee, emigrant; originally applied to the aristocrats who fled from France during the revolution of 1789-93

éminence grise   *(AY-mee-nonce greez) lit:* grey cardinal; shadowy figure of great power, the 'force behind the throne'; confidential agent; the term was originally applied to Richelieu's confessor, the Franciscan, Père Joseph

en ami   *(on ah-mee)* as a friend

en congé   *(on con-JAY)* on leave

endimanché   *(on-DEE-mon-shay)* dressed in one's Sunday best

en famille   *(on fah-MEE)* as one of the family, informally

enfant gâté   *(on-FON GAH-tay) lit:* spoilt child; the recipient of undue flattery and attention

enfant terrible   *(on-FON tehr-REE-bluh) lit:* terrible child; incorrigible child, one who is a source of embarrassment; *fig:* person whose unruliness creates difficulties

en feuilleton   *(on FOY-uh-TON)* as a pamphlet; describing a book serialized in a newspaper, etc

engagé   *(on-GAH-jay)* (politically) committed and active

en garçon   *(on gahr-SOHN)* as a bachelor

en grande tenue/en grande toilette   *(on GROND ten-EW/on GROND twa-LET)* in full regalia, in evening dress; **tenue** is more applicable to men, **toilette** is confined to women

en masse   *(on MAHS)* as a group, in force

ennui   *(ON-nwee)* boredom, restlessness, weariness induced by inactivity

ennuyé   *(on-nwee-yay)* bored, tired, weary in a state of malaise

en pantoufles	*(on PAN-too-ful) lit:* in slippers; in a relaxed manner
en passant	*(on PASS-sohn)* incidentally, in passing, by the way; a move in chess by which a pawn captures another, the latter having moved two squares forward to a position adjacent to the capturing pawn
en plein	*(on PLEN)* completely, in full; bet placed on a single number on the roulette wheel, risk taken without insurance or security
en prise	*(on PREEZ)* (in chess) piece open to immediate capture
en rapport	*(on rah-POR)* in sympathy, in agreement, seeing eye to eye
en route	*(on ROOT)* on the way; may also be used as a command, meaning start moving!
ensemble	*(on-sehm-ble)* group of people (usually gathered for a specific purpose, eg a musical **ensemble**)
entente cordiale	*(on-TONT-cor-DYAL)* friendly relationship, informal alliance between states
entêté	*see* **entêtement**
entêtement	*(on-TEH-te-mon)* obstinacy *(adj:* **entêté**)
entourloupette	*(on-TOUR-lew-PET)* underhand commercial dealing
entr'acte	*(ON-trakt) lit:* between acts; brief interlude, performance between two larger works
entrain	*(on-tren)* warmth, zest, vivacity, spirit
en train	*(on TREN)* in progress, under way
entrechat	*(ON-tray-sha)* leap in ballet in which a dancer crosses his legs more than once

entrée   *(ON-tray)* right of entry; the main course of a meal

entremets   *(ON-tray-meh) lit:* between dishes; side dish, food served between courses

entre nous   *(ON-tray noo) lit:* between us; between you and me, in confidence

entrepôt   *(ON-tray-POH)* storehouse, warehouse from which goods are distributed; port serving a large hinterland.

épater le bourgeois   *(ay-PAT-ay le BOOR-jwa) lit:* amaze the bourgeois; (deliberately) shock or embarrass the middle class (person); overturn conventionality for effect

esprit de corps   *(es-SPREE de COHR) lit:* spirit of the group; common bond between members of an institution or organization; loyalty to the gourp

esprit de l'escalier   *(es-SPREE de LESS-cal-yeh)* witty remark which is thought of too late; good retort conceived after the effect

étude   *(eh-TOOD) lit:* study; short musical composition

évolué   *(eh-vol-OO-eh) lit:* evolved; African who has adjusted to and been absorbed by European culture

expéditeur   *(ex-PEHD-ee-tuhr)* agent for the despatch of goods

extrados   *(ek-STRAH-doh)* (in architecture) the surface of an arch or vault

F

façon de parler   *(fa-SON de PAR-lay)* manner, mode of speech

fainéant   *(fay-NAY-on)* idler, do-nothing

faire sans dire (*FEHR son DEER*) *lit:* to do without speaking; *fig:* to complete a task without stressing the difficulties; to act rather than talk

fait accompli (*FEHT ac-KOM-plee*) *lit:* accomplished fact; something already undertaken or transacted

faites vos jeux (*FEHT vo-ZJUH*) *lit:* make your sport; place your bets

farceur (*fahr-SUHR*) baffoon, joker

faute de mieux (*FOHT de MEEUW*) for want of anything better; (something used as a standby) in the absence of the ideal

(les) Fauves (*lay FOHV*) *lit:* wild beasts; group of early twentieth-century French painters who rejected the conventional use of light, perspective and colour

faux bonhomme (*foh bon-OM*) *lit:* falsely good-natured man; one who hypocritically feigns good fellowship

faux dévot (*foh DAY-voh*) one who feigns peity, affectedly religious person

faux pas (*FOH pah*) *lit:* false step; social mis-step, error of taste, manners, etc

femme de chambre (*FAM de SHAM-bre*) chambermaid

femme du monde (*FAM doo MOHND*) *lit:* woman of the world; sophisticated woman

femme fatale (*FAM feh-TAHL*) *lit:* deadly woman; woman who drives her lovers to disaster; fatally fascinating woman

fête champêtre (*FEHT sham-PEHTR*) outdoor festival, rural celebration; the title of a famous painting by Giorgione

fête galante
(FEHT gah-LONT) style of painting popularized in the early eighteenth century by Antoine Watteau which featured young men and woman in theatrical costume at country festivals, etc

feu de joie
(FOY de JWA) lit: fire of joy; salute made by firing rifles, cannons, etc. on ceremonial occasions

feuilleton
(FOY-uh-TON) lit: leaflet; part of a newspaper or magazine in which prose, short works of fiction, topical essays, etc, appear

fille de joie
(FEE-ye de JWA) lit: girl of joy; euphemistic term for a prostitute

finale
(fee-NAL) concluding part of a musical piece (usually pronounced *fee-nal-AY* in English)

fin de siècle
(FAN de see-EH-cle) lit: end of century; pertaining to or characteristic of the end of the nineteenth century; decadent

finesse
(fin-NESS) delicacy; (in bridge) an attempt to win a trick when a higher card is know to be held in an opponent's hand

flèche
(flesh) lit: arrow; thin spire rising from a roof

folie de grandeur
(fol-LEE de gran-DUHR) the wish to seem great, the desire to surround oneself with the trappings of power and influence

force majeure
(FORCE mah-JUHR) irresistible force, overwhelming compulsion; (in law) the clause of a contract designed to protect the signatories against acts of God and unavoidable accidents

fracas	*(frah-kah) lit:* crash, noise; quarrel, brawl
franglais	*(fron-GLAY)* the interpolation of English words into French speech; the hybrid form of speech resulting from the mixing of English and French
frondeur	*(fron-DUHR)* malcontent, rebel, one liable to plot against the established order; derived from the *Fronde*: a series of rebellions against the established authority during the minority of Louis XIV in the 1640s

G

galimafrée	*(gal-ee-MAH-fray)* hotch-potch, jumble (often anglicized to gallimaufry)
gâteau	*(GAH-toh) lit:* cake; rich sponge, cream cake, etc
gaucherie	*(GO-sheh-ree)* awkwardness, vulgarity
genre	*(JHON-re)* style, type, school (of art, literature, etc)
gouache	*(g'wash)* painting with opaque watercolours (often thickened with gum to give the effect of painting in oils)
gourmand	*(GOOR-man)* one dedicated to ostentatious eating and entertaining, vulgar glutton, epicure
gourmandise	*(goor-mon-DEE-suh)* self-indulgence, hedonism (of the epicure)
gourmet	*(GOOR-may) lit:* wine-taster; connoisseur of wines, food, etc
grand amateur	*(grond AM-ah-tuhr)* great collector, lover of all things beautiful
grande dame	*(gronde dahm)* aristocratic lady; the term is often used to imply haughtiness or snobbery

grande passion   *(gronde PASS-y-on)* all-consuming love affair, overwhelming passion

grand Guignol   *(gron GEE-nyoll) lit:* great punch; theatrical performance consisting of a series of gruesome or macabre incidents; the term is derived from the Parisian theatre of the same name in which such entertainments were held

grand luxe   *(gron LOOCKS)* with much luxurious style

grand mal   *(gron MAL) lit:* great illness; form of epilepsy which causes the victim to lose consciousness

grand monde   *(gron MOND)* high society, stylish living

grand prix   *(gron PREE) lit:* great prize; Formula One motor racing event forming part of the world championship

(le) gratin   *((le) grah-TAHN) lit:* topping of breadcrumbs or grated cheese; upper crust of society

guerre à l'outrance   *(gerr ah LOO-trans) lit:* war to excess; war to the bitter end; *colloq:* fight to the finish

H

habitué   *(ah-BEE-tew-ay)* one who frequents a particular establishment, habitual patron of a place

haute couture   *(oat coo-TOUR)* high fashion dress-designing; the work of such dress designers

haute cuisine   *(oat kwee-ZEEN) lit:* high cooking; (the art of) fine cooking

haute école   *(oat AY-col) lit:* high school; difficult equestrian manoeuvres, complex feats of horsemanship

hauteur	*(oat-UHR)* haughty manner
haut monde	*(out MOND)* high society
homme d'affaires	*(OM daff-EHR)* businessman, legal adviser
homme de lettres	*(OM de LET-ruh)* man of letters, writer, literary man
homme d'esprit	*(OM des-SPREE)* man of sparkling wit
homme moyen sensuel	*(OM mwa-YEN SEN-swel) lit:* man of average desires; ordinary man, the typical man
honi soit qui mal y pense	*(OH-nee SWA kee MAL ee PONSE)* shame on him who thinks evil — the motto of the Order of the Garter
hors d'oeuvre	*(OR DUH-vre) lit:* outside the work; additional dish usually served before a meal

I

idée fixe	*(EE-day FEEX) lit:* fixed idea; obsession, preoccupation
idée force	*(EE-day FORS) lit:* powerful idea; notion that an idea has an active and substantive force
il a le diable au corps	*(eel ah le dee-AH-ble oh KOR)* the devil is in him; he is possessed
il a les défauts de ses qualités	*(eel ah lay day-FOH de say KAL-ee-TAY)* with his qualities, he has concomitant defects; his faults spring from his very qualities
il faut de l'argent	*(eel FOH de LAH-jon) lit:* it is necessary to have money; one must have money
immobiliste	*(im-MOH-bee-leest)* one opposed to progress, an ultra conservative (*opp:* **progressiste**)

inconnu	*(an-con-NEW)* person of unknown identity
ingénue	*(an-JAY-new)* pure and simple young woman; woman taking role of a young girl on stage
intime	*(an-TEEM)* cosy, intimate
intrados	*(an-TRAH-doh)* (in architecture) the inner side of arch, vault or arcade

J

jacquerie	*(jack-ehr-REE)* insurrection of the lower orders or peasantry; derived from a fifteenth-century peasant revolt in Northern France led by Jacques James
j'adoube	*(ja-DOOB) lit:* I adjust; (in chess) the phrase used to indicate that a player does not intend to move a piece he touches but is merely placing it correctly on its square
je ne sais quoi	*(je ne say KWA) lit:* I know not what; an indescribable something
jeu de mots	*(JUH de MO) lit:* game of words; play on words, pun
jeu d'esprit	*(JUH des-SPREE) lit:* game of the spirit; light-hearted work, witticism, literary game
jeunesse dorée	*(juh-NESS do-RAY) lit:* gilded youth; rich, fashionable young people
les jeux sont faits	*(lay JUH sohn FAY)* the bets are laid
joie de vivre	*(JWA de VEE-vru)* high spirits, enthusiasm for life
juste milieu	*(JOOST MEEL-lew)* the golden mean, the perfect balance
j'y suis, j'y reste	*(jee SWEE jee REST)* here I am, here I stay; the French Marshal, and later

President, Macmahon's statement on being asked to abandon the recently captured Malahoff Redoubt during the Crimean War

L

**laisser faire/
laissez faire**
(LESS-ehr FEHR/LESS-ay FEHR) lit: allow to do; non-action; the doctrine of governmental non-interference

**laisser passer/
laissez passer**
(LESS-ay PASS-ay) lit: allow to pass; pass, diplomat's passport

**la propriété, c'est
le vol**
(lah PROP-pree-ay-tay seh le VOLL) property is theft (Proudhon)

légèreté
(lay-JEHR-ay-tay) frivolity, levity

le roi le veut
(le RWAH le VUH) the king wishes it; it is the will of the king

lèse majesté
(LEHS MAH-zjest-ay) lit: injured sovereignty; high treason, affront to the sovereign

l'état c'est moi
(lay-TAH seh MWAH) lit: I am the state; statement attributed to Louis XIV, king of France 1643-1715

lettre de cachet
(LET-truh de ca-SHAY) warrant for arrest (in eighteenth-century France)

loi de guerre
(lwa de GERR) the laws of war; new moral code born of necessity

longueur
(lon-GUHR) lit: length; passages of tedious length in speech, writing, etc

lorgnette
(lor-NYET) eyeglass affixed to a long handle; occasionally used to denote opera glasses

louche
(LOOSH) oblique, shifty, disreputable

louvre
(LOO-vruh) (in architecture) opening with horizontal or slanted slats to form a ventilation grille

M

maison de santé	*(meh-ZON de SON-tay)* hospital or asylum (usually private)
maison de société	*(meh-ZON de SO-see-ay-tay) lit:* society house; brothel (usually used euphemistically)
maître de cuisine	*(MET-ruh de KWEE-ZEEN)* chief cook, head chef
maître d'hôtel	*(MET-ruh DOH-tell)* head waiter, steward
malaise	*(mah-LEHZ)* uneasiness, discomfort
mal du pays	*(MALL doo pez)* homesickness
mal du siècle	*(MALL doo see-ECKL)* world-weariness (usually applied to the nineteenth century)
malgré lui	*(MAL-gray LWEE)* in spite of himself, against his better judgement
mal vu	*(mal VEW)* viewed with disapproval, resented
manqué	*(mon-KAY) lit:* missed, lost, spoilt; (one who) would have achieved more in a capacity other than the one adopted
mardi gras	*(MAR-dee GRAH) lit:* fat Tuesday; carnival or festival taking place on Shrove Tuesday
matinée musicale	*(MAT-in-EH MEWS-ee-cal)* afternoon concert
mauvais goût	*(MO-vay goo)* bad taste
méchant	*(MAY shon)* naughty, spiteful
mélange	*(may-LONJE)* medley, miscellaneous mixture
mêlée	*(MEL-lay)* confused fight, scuffle, muddle

ménage	*(may-NAJE)* couple; household, domestic situation
ménage à trois	*(may-NAJE ah TRWA)* three-sided relationship; arrangement whereby husband, wife and mistress, or husband, wife and lover are under the same roof
mésalliance	*(maiz-al-ee-ahnse)* mismatch, marriage to a person of inferior social status
métier	*(MAY-tee-yay)* profession, 'calling', vocation
Métro	*(may-troh)* the subway system of Paris; abbreviation of **chemin de fer Métropolitain**
milieu	*(meel-luhr)* environment, place (in society)
mise en page	*(MEEZ on PAJ)* typographic design, layout
mise en scène	*(MEEZ en SEN)* the staging of a play; theatrical production, stage setting
misfeasance	*(MIS-fes-ahnse)* injustice or wrong judgement given by legally constituted authority
mistral	*(mees-TRAHL)* north-west wind blowing down the Rhône valley to the Mediterranean
moeurs de province	*(MUHR de pro-VONS)* provincial habits, parochial manners
mot juste	*(moh joost) lit:* right word; the word that conveys a nuance most precisely

N

nature morte	*(nah-toor mort)* still-life, artistic representation of inanimate object
néant	*(NAY-on)* emptiness, nothingness
négritude	*(nay-gree-tood)* quality of being negro;

notion of the enduring value of African culture and history; the philosophy and aesthetic developed in the 1930s by K S Senghor and Aimé Césaire as a counter to the French colonial policy of cultural assimilation

n'importe *(nam-pohrt)* it does not matter

noblesse oblige *(no-BLESS oh-BLEEGE) lit:* nobility obliges; those in high positions must be responsible

nocturne *(nok-toorn) lit:* of night; romantic musical study; night piece, painting of landscape, scene, etc, by night

nom de guerre *(NOM de GERR)* pseudonym, stage name

nom de plume *(NOM de PLOOM) lit:* pen name; pseudonym (of a writer)

nostalgie de la boue *(nos-tahl-gee de lah BOO) lit:* longing for the mud; yearning for the low life

nouveau riche *(NOU-voh REESH)* person of newly acquired wealth and status (usually used pejoratively)

nouveau roman *(NOU-voh ROH-mahn) lit:* new novel; term applied since 1955 to a group of writers (mainly French) who have wholly rejected conventional narrative forms

nouvelle vague *(NOU-vel VAHG) lit:* new wave; style of cinema adopted in France and elsewhere in the 1950s and characterized by modest budgets, a realistic approach, and relatively unknown actors

O

objet d'art *(OB jay-DAR)* work of art

objet de vertu *(OB-jay de VEHR-too) lit:* object of

quality; small work of art (enamel box, miniature, etc)

objet trouvé *(OB-jay TROO-vay) lit:* found object; beautiful or artistically valid object which is found not created; the notion of discoverable art stems from Surrealist theory

oeuvre *(UH-vr) lit:* work; the complete output of an artist

outré *(OO-tray)* improper, outrageous, unorthodox, unconventional (derived from Latin ultra: beyond)

P

papier collé *(PAP-ee-ay COL-ay) lit:* stuck paper; collage formed by sticking layers of paper on to a canvas

papier mâché *(PAP-ee-ay mah-SHAY) lit:* chewed paper; paper and glue mixed, moulded and allowed to harden

par excellence *(par ex-cel-ehnse)* above all others of a similar type, pre-eminent(ly)

par hasard *(par az-ar)* by chance

pari mutuel *(PAR-ee moot-oo-ell) lit:* mutual betting; horse racing lottery in which the total of losers' stakes on any race is divided, after the deduction of a legally fixed amount from the pool, among the winners in proportion to the amount each has staked

parti pris *(par-tee pree) lit:* party taken; partisan, having already taken sides

parvenu *(par-ven-oo)* social climber, upstart, newly rich

pas de deux *(pah de duh) lit:* step for two; dance for two people

pas possible	*(pah poss-ee-ble)* it cannot be done! it is impossible!
passé	*(PAS-say)* out of date, unfashionable, past
passe-partout	*(PASS-par-too)* skeleton key; mount for pictures
pastiche	*(pass-TEESH)* conscious imitation of the style of another
pathétique	*(pat-ay-TEEK)* with pathos, with great emotion (music)
patois	*(PAT-wa)* local dialect, indigenous form of speech; (occasionally) jargon
petit bourgeois	*(pet-ee boor-JWA)* (member of) the lower middle classes
petit mal	*(pet-ee mal)* mild form of epilepsy (usually without loss of consciousness)
pièce de résistance	*(P'YES de ray-SEES-tonse)* main dish at a meal; crowning item in a collection, performance, etc
pièce d'occasion	*(P'YES do-KAY-zhon)* work (of art, etc) composed for special occasion
pièce noire	*(P'YES nwar) lit:* black piece; dramatic form developed by Jean Anouilh based on black comedy (*see* **comédie noire**; *cf* **pièce rosée**)
pièce rosée	*(P'YES roz-ay) lit:* radiant piece; amusing piece of writing, light play, etc
pied-à-terre	*(PE-ED ah TAIR) lit:* foot on the earth; second home, residence used temporarily and for convenience
pince nez	*(panss nay) lit:* pinch nose; spectacles clipped onto the nose
piquant	*(pee-KAHN)* sharp, stinging, pointed

pirouette	*(pee-ro-WET) lit:* spinning top; dancer's spin in ballet
pis aller	*(pees allay)* the worst, last resort, makeshift, course of action pursued for want of anything better
planchette	*(PLANGH-shet)* ouija board on which the fingers rest during demonstration of psychic phenomena
plein air	*(plen err) lit:* open air; painting with quality of the outdoors; Impressionist painters strove to convey this feeling
plus ça change	*see* **plus ça change, plus c'est la même chose**
plus ça change, plus c'est la même chose	*(ploo sa shahn-je ploo seh la mehm shose)* the more something apparently changes, the more it essentially remains the same (often abbreviated to **plus ça change**)
poète maudit	*(po-ETT mo-DEE) lit:* accursed poet; poet not appreciated by his contemporaries (often used more generally than merely with reference to poets)
pointillisme	*(pwan-tee-YEZ-meh)* Impressionist method of painting using small dots of colour to heighten effect and facilitate the mixing of colours
pot pourri	*(POH poo-ree)* medley; used particularly of a mixture of herbs and spices used to scent a room
pour encourager les autres	*(poor en-coo-rahj-ay layz oatr-uh)* (punishment inflicted) to encourage the others, as a deterrent; usually used ironically, and derived from Voltaire's reference in *Candide* to the execution of Admiral Byng in 1757: 'The English shoot an admiral now and then to encourage the others'

FRENCH

pourparler	*(poor-par-lay)* discussions, negotiations
pour rendre visite	*(poor rahnd-ruh vee-zeet)* to return a call (*abbr:* **PRV**)
précis	*(PRAY-see)* summary of the content of argument, document, etc
preux chevalier	*(preuh shev-A-lee-ay) lit:* peerless knight; knight in shining armour
prix d'ami	*(PREE dah-MEE)* special concessionary price for a friend
profil perdu	*(pro-FEEL per-DOO) lit:* lost profile; profile of an object which is more than 90 degrees away from the spectator
progressiste	*(proh-GRESS-eest)* progressive (*opp:* **immobiliste**)
PRV	*see* **pour rendre visite**
puissance	*(pwee-sahnce)* power, influence, force; show-jumping event which tests a horse's jumping ability and strength over a small number of very high fences

Q

Quai d'Orsay	*(kay dor-SAY)* the site of the French foreign office in Paris; used to denote the foreign office generally
quand même	*(kahn mehm)* even enough, in spite of
qui s'excuse s'accuse	*(kee sex-kooz sah-kooz)* he who excuses himself, accuses himself

R

raconteur	*(RAH-con-TUHR)* skilled storyteller
raison d'état	*(ray-ZON day-TAH) lit:* reason of state security; used as a justification of actions

raison d'être *(ray-ZON DET-ruh) lit:* reason for being; justification, purpose

rapprochement *(rah-PROSH-mon)* re-establishment of friendly relations (especially between states)

réchauffé *(RAY-sho-FAY) adj:* reheated, warmed up; *n:* rehash, wholly unoriginal literary (or other) creation

recherché *(re-sher-SHAY)* esoteric, affected, rare

reculer pour mieux sauter *(re-KOOL-ay poor MEEUW soh-tay)* tactical withdrawal, retreat in preparation for a better opportunity

rentier *(RON-tee-eh)* one who lives off rents and investments (usually used pejoratively)

répétiteur *(ray-PET-ee-tuhr)* chorus master, prompter in opera, private tutor

répondez s'il vous plaît *(ray-pon-day seel voo pleh) lit:* please reply; please confirm or decline this invitation *(abbr:* **RSVP***)*

repoussé *(re-POO-say)* chased or embossed work

revanchiste *(re-VANGH-sheest)* political advocate of violent measures, of revenge against another nation, etc

risqué *(REES-kay)* daring, hazardous, adventurous (with an implication of indelicacy)

rites de passage *(REET duh pas-SAHG)* important landmarks in a person's life

roman à cléf *(ro-MAHN ah CLAY) lit:* novel with a key; a novel in which real people figure under fictitious names

roman fleuve *(ro-MAHN FLUHV) lit:* river novel; novel which charts the progress of a group or family over several generations

roué	*(ROO-eh)* rake, profligate
RSVP	*see* **répondez s'il vous plaît**

S

salon	*(sah-long)* drawing room; gathering of intellectuals, writers, politicans, etc in such
sans culotte	*(song COO-lot) lit:* without breeches; mob insurrectionist; the term was applied to the mainly Parisian working class groups who supported the revolution of 1789-93
sans gêne	*(song jehn) lit:* without restraint; failing to recognize constraints, making oneself at home
sans pareil	*(song PAR-ehy)* without equal, incomparable
sans peine	*(song pen)* without difficulty, easily
sans souci	*(song SOO-see) lit:* without care; without concern, worry, etc
sauve qui peut	*(soav kee puh)* run for your life; every man for himself
savoir faire	*(sav-wahr fehr)* know-how, sophistication, self-confidence
savoir vivre	*(sav-wahr VEEV-ruh)* to know how to live; elegance, social grace, good breeding
séance	*(say-ahnce) lit:* sitting, session; group meeting in attempt to contact spirits, etc
sens intime	*(sons en-TEEM) lit:* intimate meaning; inner meaning of a passage, etc
si jeunesse savait, si vieillesse pouvait	*(see JUH-ness sah-veh see VYAY-esse poo-veh)* if the young only knew, if the old only could

simpliste	*(sam-PLEEST)* too simple, suspiciously easy
sobriquet	*(soh-bree-KAY)* nickname, false name
soi disant	*(SWA DEE-sohn)* self-styled, would-be, so-called
soigné	*(SWAH-nyeh)* well-executed (production, design, etc); well-groomed (person)
son et lumière	*(son eh LOO-mee-yerr) lit:* sound and light; displays incorporating lighting, music, narrative, etc
soupçon	*(soop-SOHN) lit:* suspicion, conjecture; small quantity, dash (of garlic, pepper, etc)
succès de scandale	*(suk-SEH de scan-DAHL)* success bred of the scandal accompanying the performance of a work
succès d'estime	*(suk-SEH des-TEEM)* critical success, work (of art) favoured by critics but not by the general public

T

tableau	*(tah-BLO)* picture, picturesque representation of event, etc
tableaux	*(tah-BLO)* sequence of pictures outlining an event
table d'hôte	*(tah-ble doht) lit:* host's table; set meal served at a standard price and a fixed time in hotel, guest house, etc (*cf:* **à la carte**)
tachisme	*(tash-EESM)* form of abstract art in which paint is randomly splashed or sprayed on to a canvas
tant pis, tant mieux	*(ton PEE ton MYUH)* so much the worse, so much the better, it can't be helped (expression of resignation)

touché	*(too-SHAY) lit:* touched; well hit; on the mark, signifies a successful stroke in a fencing match, or a comment that successfully concludes an argument
tour ɑe force	*(TOUR de FORCE)* display of technical virtuosity, powerful exhibition of skill
tout comprendre c'est tout pardonner	*(too KOM-pren seh too par-don-eh)* to understand everything is to pardon everything
tout court	*(too COOR)* without further explanation or description
tout de suite	*(too SWEET)* immediately
tout ensemble	*(toot en-sehm-ble)* all together, in unison
tout vient à qui sait attendre	*(too vyen ah kee set ah-ten-dr)* everything comes to him who waits
trompe l'oeil	*(TROMP l'OY) lit:* deceive the eye; effect in painting, sculpture or architecture achieved by optical illusion

V

ventre à terre	*(ven re ah ter) lit:* belly to the ground; at top speed very fast
vérité	*(vay-ree-TAY)* realism in TV, film, etc (*see* **cinéma vérité**)
vers de société	*(ver do soh-see-ay-tay)* light, topical, often satirical, verse
vers libre	*(ver leeb-re) lit:* free verse; poetry without orthodox structure, rhythm or rhyme pattern
vie manquée	*(VEE mon-KAY)* misdirected life
vis-à-vis	*(VEEZ-ah-VEE)* concerning, with regard to, relating to
vogue la galère	*(voag la GA-LER) lit:* let the galley sail freely; let's chance it

voilà   *(vwa-la) lit:* look there; look at that

vol au vent   *(vol-oh-ven)* pastry filled with meat or fish, vegetables, sauce, etc

volte face   *(VOL-te FASS)* reversal of opinion, about-face, repudiation of a previous situation

German

Few German phrases are used in English, and those which are tend to be restricted to philosophy. However, words such as *Zeitgeist, Schadenfreude* and *Weltanschauung* are widely used, and many important artistic terms are taken from German.

Pronunciation

a	may be short or long and the text should be followed
b	is as in English except at the end of a word when it is pronounced *p*
ch	is soft, as in *loch*
chs	is pronounced *x*
d	is as in English, except at the end of a word when it is pronounced *t*
e	may be short or long and the text should be followed
g	is as in English except at the end of a word when it is pronounced *ch*
ei	is always pronounced *eye*
ie	is always pronounced *ee*
o	may be short or long and the text should be followed
j	is pronounced as *y* in English
q	is pronounced as *kv*
r	is rolled
s	is hard (similar to *z* in English) except at the end of a word
sch	is pronounced without the *c*
th	the *h* is silent
tz	the *z* is soft
u	may be short or long and the text should be followed

| **v** | ɪs pronounced *f* |
| **w** | ɪs pronounced *v* |

umlauts (ä, ö and *ü)* alter vowel sounds and the phonetics adopted
in the text should be followed

Note:
*All German nouns have capital letters and are capitalized here,
though in English usage capitalization is often optional.*

A

Absicht *(AP-zict)* (in psychology) purpose, intention

Achtung *(ahk-TUHNG)* (as military command) attention!

Aktiengesellschaft *(ak-tee-en ge-ZELL-shaft)* limited company

Angst *(ahngst)* (feeling of) dread, anxiety, guilt

Anschluss *(AHN-shlus)* union, joining; used especially to refer to the annexation of Austria by Hitler in 1938

Aufklärung *(owf-KLEH-rung) lit:* enlightenment; the Enlightenment (of the eighteenth century)

auf Wiedersehen *(owf VEE-der-zehn)* until we see each other again

Ausländer *(OWS-len-der)* foreigner, alien; the use of the term is often pejorative, with a connotation of boorishness

Autobahn *(OW-toh BAHN)* German motorway

B

Baedeker *(BAY-deck-er)* guidebook; originally referring to the guidebooks written by Baedeker, but now used with reference to any travel guide

Bauhaus *(BOW-hows)* architecture and design school of the early twentieth century;

used as an adjective to describe the modern, 'international' style

Bergschrund *(BERG-shroond)* the crevasse between an ice sheet and the sides of a valley

Berufsverbot *(be-ROOFS-ver-BOHT)* law prohibiting people considered politically unsuitable from entering public service

Biedermeierstil *(bee-der-MY-er-shteel)* simple, unostentatious artistic style current in Central Europe in the first half of the nineteenth century

Bierkeller *(BEER-kel-ler)* beer cellar

Bildungsroman *(BILL-doohngs-ro-MAN) lit:* formation novel; novel tracing the chronological history and psychological development of a single character (eg *Tom Jones, David Copperfield,* etc)

Blaue Reiter *(BLAU-we RY-ter) lit:* blue horsemen; title of a journal in Germany in 1911-14, and a term applied to a group of expressionist artists, including the composer Alfred Schoenberg

Blitzkrieg *(BLITZ-kreeg)* lightning warfare, sudden and devastating strike; associated historically with the form of attack adopted by the German forces in Western Europe in 1939-40; 'blitz' was also used to describe bombing raids of civilian areas

Bräu *(brow)* brew

die Brücke *(dee BREW-ke) lit:* the Bridge; the collective term for a group of German expressionist artists in the early years of the twentieth century; work in this style

Bundesrepublik *(BOON-des-re-pub-leek)* Federal Republic of Germany, ie West Germany

Bundestag	*(BOON-des-tag)* federal assembly of West Germany; lower house of West German Parliament

D

Danke schön	*(DAN-ke SHUHN)* many thanks
Dasein	*(DAH-zyn)* existence, being, presence
Ding an sich	*(DING an ZICH) lit:* the thing in itself, the reality behind the surface appearance
Doppelgänger	*(DOP-pul-GENG-er) lit:* double; spirit accompanying a person and seemingly identical in form; a common image in Romantic poetry
Drang nach Osten	*(DRAHNG nach OS-ten)* impulse towards the east; national aggrandizement by eastward extension of boundaries
Dummkopf	*(DUHM-kopf)* blockhead, extremely stupid person

E

Einstellung	*(EYN-shtel-lung) lit:* set, attitude; (in psychology) fixed response to a problem
das Ende vom Lied	*(das EN-de fom LEED) lit:* the end of the song; the upshot, the end of the matter
Erdgeist	*(EHRD-gyst)* earth spirit
Erlkönig	*(EHRL-kuh-nig)* elf king, mischievous spirit
ersatz	*(EHR-zatz) lit:* replacement; substitute, imitation (usually inferior)
Ewigweibliche	*(AY-vig vyb-lich-uh)* the eternal feminine, the power of women to spiritualize mankind

Expressionismus *(ecκ-SPRES-shun-IZ-mus)* (tne art movement of) Expressionism

F

Festschrift *(FEST-shrift) lit:* festival writing; a volume of essays presented in commemoration of a distinguished scholar (usually marking some occasion in his life)

Frau *(FROW)* woman, lady, wife

Fräulein *(FROY-lyn)* unmarried young lady

Führer *(FEW-rer)* leader; title assumed by Adolf Hitler in 1934

Führerprinzip *(FEW-rer-print-SEEP) lit:* principle of leadership; notion of unlimited authority on which Hitler's regime was based

G

Gastarbeiter *(GAST-ahr-BYE-ter) lit:* guest worker; worker of foreign nationality (working in Germany)

Gauleiter *(GOW-ly-ter)* head of Nazi party at province level (*colloq:* petty tyrant)

geflügelte Worte *(ge-FLEW-gel-tuh VOR-tuh) lit:* winged words; pamphlets published in support of various sides of an issue

Geist *(gyst) lit:* ghost, spirit, soul (of individual, nation, era, etc)

Geistesgeschichte *(GYST-es-ge-SHIK-te) lit:* history of the spirit; history of ideas, cultural history

Geisteswissen-schaften *(GYST-es-VISS-en-shaf-ten) lit:* sciences of the spirit; notion that certain characteristics pervade every facet of cultural and intellectual life

Geld	*(gelt)* money
Gemeinschaft	*(ge-MYN-shaft)* association based on love or kinship (*cf* **Gesellschaft**)
Gemüt	*(ge-MEWT)* temperament; impact of an emotional experience
gemütlich	*(ge-MEWT-lich)* leisurely, comfortably
Gemütlichkeit	*(ge-MEWT-lich-kyt)* geniality, good-fellowship, cosiness
Gesamtkunstwerk	*(ge-ZAMT-koonst-VERK)* work of art regarded as a totality (eg combination of the music and libretto of an opera)
Gesellschaft	*(ge-ZELL-shaft)* company, society, association, organization based on self-interest and contractual agreement (*cf* **Gemeinschaft**)
Gesellschaft mit beschränkter Haftung	*(ge-ZELL-shaft mit be-SHRANK-ter HAF-tung)* private limited liability company (*abbr:* **GmbH**)
Gestalt	*(ge-SHTALT)* shape, form, totality; a school of psychoanalysis which seeks to focus on the shape of the whole personality
Gestapo	*(ge-SHTA-po)* German secret police (under Hitler); term is applied to organizations similar to this in severity and in methods of operation
Gesundheit	*(ge-ZUHND-hyt) lit:* (may you) be restored to health; good health (often used after someone has sneezed)
GmbH	*see* **Gesellschaft mit beschränkter Haftung**
Götterdämmerung	*(GUH-ter-DEHM-er-ung)* twilight of the gods; title of an opera by Richard Wagner

Gruppe	*(GROO-pe)* group, association (of artists, writers, etc)

H

Handbuch	*(HANT-buk)* manual, guide, handbook
Hausfrau	*(HOWS-frow) lit:* woman of the house; housewife
Herrenvolk	*(HER-en-FAULK)* master race; the Nazi term for the German people
Hinterland	*(HIN-ter-LANT)* interior of a country, backwoods; often used in English to describe an area served by a major port or city

J

jawohl	*(ya-VOL)* yes, certainly; strong affirmative
Jugendstil	*(YOO-gent-shteel) lit:* the style of youth; modern art; derived from an arts magazine which first appeared in 1896
Junker	*(YOON-ker)* Prussian aristocrat, member of Prussian landowning class

K

kaputt	*(kah-POOT)* ruined, smashed, broken
Kirche, Küche, Kinder	*(KEER-shuh, KOO-shuh, KIN-duh)* church, kitchen, children; German nationalist concept of the proper interests of the German woman
Kitsch	*(kitsch) lit:* trash; (something which is) self-consciously vulgar, meretricious, etc
Kriegspiel	*(KREEG-shpeel) lit:* war game; form of chess in which each player sees only his side of the board and works out his opponent's position from information, passed on by an umpire, regarding the

legality of his moves and the pieces which are taken

Kultur *(kul-TOOR)* culture, civilization (with overtones of supposed racial superiority)

Kulturgeschichte *(kul-TOOR-guh-SHIK-tuh)* history of culture or civilization

Kulturkampf *(kul-TOOR-kampf)* struggle over social institutions between Church and State (especially that in the 1870s between Bismarck and the Catholic Church in the newly united Germany)

Kulturschande *(KUL-toor-SHAN-duh)* insult to good taste; crime against civilization

Kulturwissenschaft *see* **Wissenschaft**

Künstlerroman *(KOON-stler-ro-MAN) lit:* artist novel; novel tracing the development of an artist's sensibility

L

Lebe hoch *(LEH-be HOACH)* to your health! cheers!

Lebensraum *(LAY-bens-ROWM) lit:* living space; Germany attempted to justify its policy of territorial aggrandizement after Hitler had come to power in 1933 by arguing that it needed more **Lebensraum**

Lehranalyse *(LAYR-an-al-y-ZE)* teaching analysis; process in which Freudian psychologists are themselves analysed as part of their training

Lehrstück *(LAYR-shtook) lit:* moral tale; form of theatre, championed by Bertolt Brecht in the 1930s, the intention of which was to instruct the performer (ie not necessarily to entertain or instruct the audience)

Leitmotiv *(LYT-mo-TEEF) lit:* leading motive; theme associated with a person or situation; recurrent theme within school or genre (particularly in music)

Liebchen	*(LEEB-shen)* love, sweetheart
Lied	*(leed)* song, poem, ballad
Lieder	*(LEED-er)* song-cycle, series of musical ballads
Lorelei	*(LOR-eh-lye)* (in German legend) siren, woman who leads men to their destruction
Luftwaffe	*(LOOFT-va-fuh)* airforce (specifically that of the Third **Reich**)
Lumpenproletariat	*(LOOM-pen-pro-leh-TAY-ree-at)* the ragged, common people; amorphous social group below the proletariat, consisting of beggars, tramps, etc; term used in Marxist theory to denote those indifferent to the cause of revolution because of lack of education, organization, structure and class consciousness

M

Machtpolitik	*(macht-PO-li-TEEK)* lit: politics of might, power politics; notion that power governs international relations and the conduct of foreign policy
Meisterstück	*(MY-ster-SHTOOK)* masterpiece, key work (of an artist's output), masterwork (*see* **Meisterwerk**)
Meisterwerk	*(MY-ster-VERK)* masterpiece, chief work

N

Naturwissenschaft	*see* **Wissenschaft**
Neue Künstlervereinigung	*(NOY-e KOON-stler-fer-EYN-i-gung) lit:* new association of artists; Munich-based group which was in the vanguard of abstract and Expressionist painting before World War I

Neue Sachlichkeit	*(NOY-e ZACH-lich-kyt) lit:* new objectivity; term describing the growth of functionalism in architecture and naturalism in art in Germany in the 1920s

O

Oktoberfest	*(ok-TOE-ber-fest)* beer festival (traditional in West Germany and parts of the United States)
Ostpolitik	*(OST-po-li-TEEK) lit:* Eastern politics; term describing German Chancellor Willy Brandt's policy in the early 1970s, which aimed at establishing better relations with the Eastern European countries

P

Panzer	*(PANT-ser) lit:* coat of mail; heavily armoured tank corps
Putsch	*(pootsh)* insurrection, attempted revolution

R

Realpolitik	*(ray-AL-po-li-TEEK)* (notion of) politics based on realism not idealism; pragmatic politics
Reich	*(RYK)* state, empire (Hitler's regime styled itself the Third **Reich)**
Reichstag	*(RYCH-stag)* parliament, legislative body

S

Schadenfreude	*(SHAH-den-FROY-duh)* malicious joy at another's misfortune
Schauspiel	*(SHOW-speel)* spectacle

Schlaraffenland	*(shlar-AHF-en-lant)* fool's paradise
Schweinhund	*(SCHWYN-hoont) lit:* pig dog; villain, blackguard
Schwerpunkt	*(SHVEHR-poonkt)* the main thrust (of an argument, etc)
Sehnsucht	*(ZAYN-zookt)* longing, nostalgia
Sieg Heil	*(zeeg HYL) lit:* hail victory; chant adopted by masses at Nazi rallies
Stammlokal	*(SHTAM-lo-KAL) lit:* root locality; area forming part of the regular pattern of the lives of a person or group
Stammtisch	*(SHTAM-tish)* table (in pub, restaurant etc) regularly occupied by a group of friends or associates
stimmt	*(shtimmt)* correct; precisely
Sturm	*(shturhm) lit:* storm; collective term for the varied manifestations of the Expressionist movement in Berlin
Sturm und Drang	*(SHTURHM unt DRAHNG)* storm and struggle; emotional turmoil (used to describe the early Romantic period in German literature)

U

Ubermensch	*(OO-ber-mensh)* superman

V

verboten	*(fehr-BOH-ten)* forbidden, prohibited, illegal
Verklärung	*(fehr-KLAI-rung)* transfiguration, transformation
Vollmacht	*(FOLL-mahkt)* full power, proxy, power of attorney

W

Wahrheit und Dichtung   *(VAR-hyt unt DICH-tung)* truth and poetry

Wandel der Zeiten   *(VAHN-del dehr TSY-ten) lit:* the changeability of time; times (values, ways of life, etc) change (expression of regret)

Wanderer   *(VAHN-de-rer)* wanderer, traveller; common image in Romantic literature, with the implication that the traveller is seeking discovery

Wanderjahre   *(VAHN-der-YAH-ruh)* years of travel; originally denoting the journeyman's itinerant life before advancing to mastership, now used far more generally to refer to a person's years of experiment prior to settling into a career, etc

Wanderlust   *(VAHN-der-loost)* desire to travel, urge to wander (usually used to imply extreme restlessness)

Wehrmacht   *(VEHR-mahkt) lit:* defensive force; the armed forces of the Third **Reich**

Weltanschauung   *(VELT-an-SHAU-ung)* world-view, philosophy of life, total philosophical scheme

Weltburger   *(VELT-bur-ger)* citizen of the world, international figure

Weltgeist   *(VELT-gyst)* spirit of the world, spirit of the age, prevailing temper of the times

Weltlust   *(VELT-loost)* worldly pleasure, hedonism

Weltmann   *(VELT-mahn)* man of the world, cosmopolitan character

Weltpolitik   *(VELT po-li-TEEK)* the practice of politics on a global scale

Weltschmerz	*(VELT-shmehrtz) lit:* grief of the world; distress at the world situation, world-weariness, complete pessimism
Wissenschaft	*(VISS-sen-shaft)* science, knowledge; often employed with an adjectival prefix, as in **Kulturwissenschaft**: the study of culture; and **Naturwissenschaft**: the study of natural science
Wunderkind	*(VOON-der-kint) lit:* wonder child; infant prodigy, child achieving some kind of success or repute

Z

Zeitgeist	*(TSYT-guyst)* spirit of the time; (used particularly to describe) the literature or philosophy of a period
Zeitnot	*(TSYT-note)* shortage of time, slavery to the clock
Zollverein	*(TSOL-fer-yn) lit:* customs association; free trade area (established in most of Germany in 1815 and tying the northern and central German states to Prussia)

Italian

Italian phrases in English are related principally to music and art. Occasionally, it has been difficult to draw the line between terms in common use and words derived from Italian but not widely used in English, and we have excluded terms which we considered fully absorbed into English.

Pronunciation

a	is long (as in f*a*ther in English)
c	is pronounced *k* before *a, o, u* and all consonants, and is pronounced *ch* before *e* and *i*
e	may be open or closed and the text should be followed
h	is never pronounced, but when placed between *c* and *e, c* and *i, g* and *e,* and *g* and *i* changes the *c* to *k* and makes the *g* hard
i	is pronounced as *ee* in *fee*
g	is hard before *a*, o and *u*, and soft before *e* and *i*
gli	*g* is silent and the combination is pronounced like *lli* in English mi*lli*ons
gn	pronounced like the *n* in *n*ews
o	may be open or closed and the text should be followed
q	is always followed by *u* and pronounced *kw*
r	should be rolled and distinctly pronounced
s	is soft when it occurs between two vowels
sce **sci**	is pronounced *sh*
sche **schi**	pronounced as *sk* in English
u	is long, like *oo* in f*oo*l
z	may be hard or soft and the text should be followed

A

a capella *(ah ca-PEL-lah)* (music) without accompaniment; choral singing

accelerando *(a-cheh-leh-RAHN-doh)* (in music) gradually gathering speed

acciaccatura *(a-chah-ka-TOO-rah)* grace note played quickly before essential note of a melody

adagio *(a-DAH-joh)* slow(ly); (in music) movement in slow time

affettuoso *(ah-fet-TU-oh-soh)* (in music) with feeling

aggiornamento *(a-JOR-na-MEN-toh)* modernization

a giorno *(ah JOR-no) lit:* like daylight; (idiom meaning) up to date

agitato *(a-jee-TAH-toh)* agitated, emotional; (in music) very fast tempo

al dente *(al DEN-tay) lit:* to the tooth; not overcooked, still hard when eaten (usually used with reference to pasta)

alla breve *(al-a BREH-veh)* concise; (in music) quick time

alla prima *(al-a PREE-mah) lit:* first; painting rapidly and without subsequent retouching

allargando *(al-ar-GAN-doh)* (in music) slowing down gradually

allegretto   *(al-leh-GRET-toh)* (in music) moderately slow tune; somewhat slower than **allegro**

allegrissimo   *(al-leh-GRIS-si-moh)* (in music) very fast time

allegro   *(a-LEH-groh)* (in music) brisk, happy

allegro ma non troppo   *(a-LEH-groh mah non TRO-poh)* (in music) briskly but not too fast

a mezza voce   *(ah MEH-tsa VOH-chay) lit:* at half voice; softly

andante   *(an-DAHN-teh) lit:* walking; slow tempo (in flowing style)

andantino   *(an-dahn-TEE-no)* (in music) moderately slow time; somewhat slower than **andante**

appassionato   *(ah-pahs-syoh-NAH-toh)* (in music) with passion, with great feeling

appoggiatura   *(ahp-POH-djah-TOO-rah)* accented dissonant note in a melody

a prima vista   *(ah PREE-ma VEE-stah)* at first sight, at first glance

aria   *(AH-ree-ah)* song for a single voice in an opera

arioso   *(a-ree-O-soh)* free, narrative singing; extremely melodious speech

arpeggio   *(ar-PAY-joh)* chord played in (usually rapid, upward) succession, broken chord

arricciato   *(ah-ree-CHAH-toh)* layer of paint which affords a smooth surface for the drawing and painting of a **fresco**

arrivederci   *(ah-ree-veh-DER-chee)* farewell, until we meet again

assai   *(as-SAH-ee)* very (usually in music)

a tempo   *(ah TEM-poh)* (in music) in time

B

bambino *(bam-BEE-noh)* infant, child

basso continuo *(BAHS-so con-TIN-u-oh)* figured bass line, composed at the keyboard (occasionally employed metaphorically with reference to adroit extemporization)

basso profundo *(BAHS-so pro-FOON-doh)* (in music) very deep bass voice

basta *(BAH-stah)* enough! stop it!

bel canto *(bel CAN-toh) lit:* beautiful singing; singing with full, rich tone; **virtuoso** singing

ben trovato *(ben tro-VAH-toh) lit:* well found; ingenious invention (also used as an exclamation)

bozzetto *(boh-TSEH-toh) lit:* sketch; first draft, initial design (of painting, sculpture, etc)

brio *(BREE-yoh)* spirit, vivacity

buffo *(BOO-foh)* comic, burlesque (may be used as a noun or an adjective)

C

cadenza *(cah-DEN-zah)* elaborate (sometimes improvised) solo performance near the end of a larger musical work

calando *(cal-LAHN-doh) lit:* going down; (in music) softer and slower, fading away

cantabile *(can-TAH-bee-lay) lit:* which can be sung; (in music) smooth and flowing style, seemingly effortless singing

cantata *(can-TAH-tah) lit:* which has been sung; choral work

cappuccino	*(cah-poo-CHEE-noh)* coffee with milk and a sprinkling of grated chocolate
capriccio	*(cah-PREE-cho) lit:* caprice, whim; (in music) lively, impulsively; (in art) work of lively imagination
cinquecento	*(CHIN-kweh-CHEN-toh)* the sixteenth century
cognoscenti	*(koh-nyo-SHEN-tee) lit:* connoisseurs; experts in any field
coloratura	*(kol-orr-a-TOO-rah) lit:* colouring (of passage in music); brilliant singing, with passages designed to display virtuosity (usually used adjectivally in English)
commedia dell'arte	*(com-MEHD-ya del ART-ay)* extempore comic drama performed by travelling players in Italy from the sixteenth century and using stock characters such as Pierrot and Harlequin
con brio	*(con BREE-oh)* (in music) with spirit, with great life and vivacity
concertante	*(con-cher-TAHN-tay)* (music) designed to display the virtuosity of several players
con dolore	*(con doh-LOHR-ay)* (in music) dolefully, mournfully
condottiere	*(con-doh-TYEH-ray)* leader of mercenaries
con fuoco	*(con FWO-coh) lit:* with fire; (in music) fiery, spirited
con moto	*(con MO-toh) lit:* with movement; (in music) with life
con spirito	*(con SPEE-ree-toh)* (in music) with spirit
contralto	*(coh-TRAHL-toh)* lowest female voice; singer with such a voice
contraposto	*(con-trah-POHS-toh) lit:* juxtaposed;

(sculpture or painting of a figure) in an absurd or unlikely pose

crescendo *(creh-SHEN-doh) lit:* growing; (in music) increasing in volume

D

di bravura *(dee brah-VOO-rah) lit:* with bravado; (in music) with virtuosity, with great skill

dilettante *(deel-eh-TAN-tay) lit:* amateur; lover of the arts; one who approaches subjects without application or serious study

diminuendo *(dee-mee-new-EN-doh) lit:* diminishing; (in music) gradual decrease in sound

divertimento *(dee-ver-ti-MEN-toh)* (in music) light instrumental work; (in general) a pleasing diversion

dolce far niente *(DOL-che far NYEN-tay) lit:* gentle inactivity; blissful idleness

la dolce vita *(lah DOL-che VEE-tah)* the good life (often has pejorative overtones in English)

E

eppur si muove *(eh-POOR si MWO-ve) lit:* and yet it moves; Galileo's alleged remark after his recantation; used now as an exclamation of frustration in the face of narrow-minded or obstinate clinging to erroneous ideas

estro poetico *(ES-troh po-ET-ee-koh)* the imagination of poets

F

falsetto *(fall-SET-toh)* voice above the natural register of the singer

finita la commedia   *(fin-EE-tah la com-MED-yah)* the farce is over, the game is up

forte   *(FOR-tay)* (in music) strong, loud; strong point, principal ability (of person)

fortepiano   *(for-tay-pee-AHN-oh) lit:* loud and soft; early name for **pianoforte**

fortissimo   *(for-TIS-see-moh)* (in music) very loud

fresco   *(FRES-coh) lit:* fresh; method of painting applying watercolour to dry plaster (**fresco secco**) or prepared plaster (**fresco buon**)

fresco buon   *see* **fresco**

fresco secco   *see* **fresco**

frizzante   *(free-ZAHN-tay)* piquant, sparkling, stinging (usually of wine)

G

glissando   *(glee-SAHN-doh)* (in music) sliding from one note to another, easy transition between notes

(il) gran rifiuto   *(grahn ree-FYEW-toh)* the great refusal; derived from Celestine V's eventual refusal to accept papal office, but used with reference to the refusal of any honour or office

gran turismo   *(grahn too-REES-moh)* sports car designed to seat two people comfortably (*abbr:* **GT**)

grave   *(GRAH-vay)* (in music) solemn, slow

gregario   *(greh-GAR-yoh)* camp follower, private retainer

grottesca   *(gro-TESS-kah)* decoration with humans and animals intertwined in foliage; elaborate tangle

GT *see* **gran turismo**

I

illuminati *(il-loo-me-NAH-tee) lit:* enlightened; (those) possessing enlightenment and wisdom

impasto *(im-PAHS-toh)* thickness of paint on canvas

imprimitura *(im-PREE-mee-TOO-rah)* prepared surface of a canvas

inamorato/ inamorata *(in-a-mo-RA-toh/in-am-o-RA-tah)* one who is in love

incognito *(in-cog-NEE-toh)* unknown (person), anonymous (usually used as an adverb in English)

infingardo *(een-feen-GAHR-doh)* lazy, slothful (often used in the corrupt noun form infingard)

intermezzo *(een-tayr-MEH-tsoh) lit:* in between; (in music) interlude, short movement connecting major divisions of larger work

L

larghetto *(lar-GHAY-toh)* (in music) relatively slow time; less slow than **largo**

largo *(LAR-goh)* (in music) very slow and broad

legato *(lay-GAH-toh)* (in music) fluent(ly), uninterrupted(ly), without breaks between notes

lento *(LEN-toh)* slow(ly)

lingua franca *(LEEN-gwa FRAN-ka) lit:* frankish tongue; common tongue, used for communication between people from different countries

literati   *(lee-teh-RAH-tee)* educated and well-read (people)

loggia   *(lodg-ya) lit:* lodge; gallery open (often pillared) on one or more sides

M

maestoso   *(mah-ess-TOH-soh)* (in music) majestically, with dignity

maestro   *(mah-ESS-troh)* master, principal, teacher, conductor of orchestra; used as a title for eminent musicians

mafia   *(MAH-fee-yah) lit:* bragging; opposition to authority often manifested in crime; (name of an) international criminal conspiracy (though often applied to any criminal group)

magnifico   *(mah-NYEE-fee-koh)* great man, grandee; often used to denote a caricature or stereotype, as in the **commedia dell'arte**

ma non troppo *(mah non TROH-poh)* (in music) not too much

mesto   *(MEH-stoh)* (in music) sad, melancholy

mezza voce *(MEH-tsa VOH-cheh) lit:* in medium voice; at medium volume

mezzo   *(MEH-tsoh) lit:* half; moderate(ly)

mezzo soprano *(MEH-tso sop-RAN-oh)* the female voice between **contralto** and **soprano**

modello   *(moh-DEL-loh)* detailed outline or sketch, model; formerly referred to small-scale rendering of a painting submitted to a patron, but now in more general use

molto   *(MOL-toh)* much, very

morbidezza   *(mor-bee-day-tsah) lit:* tenderness; extreme delicacy in style of painting (usually used pejoratively)

O

obligato   *(oh-blee-GAH-toh)* indispensable instrumental accompaniment

ogni tanto   *(OHN-yee TAHN-toh)* now and then, occasionally

P

parlando   *(par-LAHN-do) lit:* speaking; (singing) with distinct enunciation

partita   *(par-TEE-tah)* sweet, (such a) movement in a musical work

penseroso   *(pen-seh-RO-soh)* thinker, usually with a melancholic disposition

pentimento   *(pen-tee-MEN-toh) lit:* repentance; detail effaced which comes into view with the passage of time (usually refers to a mark left by a painter's erasure or alteration)

pianissimo   *(pee-ahn-ISS-ee-moh)* (in music) very softly

piano   *(pee-AHN-oh)* (in music) soft(ly)

pianoforte   *(pee-ahn-o-FOR-tay) lit:* soft and loud; formal term for piano; *see* **fortepiano**

piazza   *(pee-AHT-tsah)* public square, courtyard, marketplace; verandah

pietà   *(pee-ay-TAH) lit:* pity; picture of the dead Christ in the lap of the Virgin Mary

pizzicato   *(pee-tzee-CAH-toh) lit:* plucked; indication that string players should pluck not bow their instruments

politico	*(po-LEE-tee-coh)* politician, opportunist; usually used sarcastically or ironically in English to suggest a person obsessed by the mundane mechanics of politics
predella	*(preh-DEL-lah)* the painted or carved panel below an altarpiece; decorative panel beneath any picture
prestissimo	*(preh-STEE-see-moh)* (in music) very, very fast
presto	*(PREH-sto)* quickly; (in music) very fast tempo
prima donna	*(PREE-ma DOH-nah)* leading female singer in an opera; may be used pejoratively in English to signify a proud, vain or selfish person
primo	*(PREE-moh)* first part (in a duet, etc)
primo basso	*(PREE-mo BAHS-soh)* (in music) chief bass
putto	*(POO-toh)* figure of a cherub or child

Q

quadratura	*(KWA-drah-TOO-rah)* perspective paintings in a room, designed to deceive the eye
quattrocento	*(kwat-troh-CHEN-toh)* the fifteenth century; denotes the Renaissance and especially Italian Renaissance style

R

rallentando	*(RAHL-len-TAHN-doh)* lit: slowing down; (in music) diminishing in speed
recitativo	*(reh-chee-tah-TEE-voh)* spoken part of an opera
refacimento	*(ree-fach-i-MEN-toh)* recasting,

remaking, rehash

relievo
(ree-le-EH-voh) lit: relief; describing the depth of a carving or sculpture (ie the distance of a design from a plane); relief may be high, medium, **stiacciato** (scratched or etched), or **cavo** (inverted)

relievo cavo
see **relievo**

relievo stiacciato
see **relievo**

Risorgimento
(ree-SOR-gee-MEN-toh) lit: resurgence; the movement for Italian unification in the nineteenth century

ritenuto
(ree-teh-NOO-toh) (in music) immediately slowly, subsequent passage to be slower

rubato
(roo-BAH-toh) lit: robbed; (in music) expressive; deviation from strict time

S

salto mortale
(SAL-to mor-TAH-lay) lit: somersault; critical moment, climacteric

scherzando
(skert-ZAHN-doh) lit: joking(ly); (in music) in a lively manner, briskly

scherzo
(SKER-tzoh) lit: joke; lively, playful piece or manner; fast, joyful movement in concerto, etc

sforzando
(sfor-TSAND-oh) lit: forcing; sudden emphasis, usually followed immediately by a reversion to previous level

sfumato
(sfoo-MAH-toh) lit: evaporated; style of painting in which differences of colour and light are indistinct

soprano
(so-PRAH-noh) highest female or boy's singing voice

sostenuto
(sos-ten-EW-toh) (in music) sustained,

smooth and fluent

sprezzatura   *(SPREH-tsa-TOO-rah)* nonchalance, effortless technique

staccato   *(stah-CAH-toh)* (in music) disconnected, (played in) detached manner

stretto   *(STREH-toh) lit:* narrow; (in music) quicker time; passage in a fugue where the subject overlaps its answer

T

tempera   *(TEM-peh-rah)* (method of) painting with egg-based pigments (now largely synthetic)

tempo giusto   *(TEM-po JEW-stoh)* (in music) strict time

terrazzo   *(teh-RAHT-zoh)* terrace

tessitura   *(tes-see-TOO-rah)* natural range of a voice or instrument

toccata   *(toh-KA-tah)* keyboard music displaying the virtuosity of the performer

trattoria   *(tra-tor-REE-ah)* relatively inexpensive restaurant

troppo   *(TROH-poh)* too much; *see* **ma non troppo**

U

uomo universale   *(WO-mo oo-nee-vehr-SAL-ay) lit:* universal man; man of many talents, 'Renaissance man'

V

vedutista   *(VEH-doo-TEES-tah)* painter specializing in realistic scenes; anyone who depicts such scenes in whatever medium or in speech

verismo   *(vehr-EEZ-moh)* realism, objectivity

vertù   *(vehr-TOO) lit:* virtue; love of fine arts

vibrato   *(vee-BRA-toh)* tremulous variation of notes in music or speech

virtuoso   *(vur-too-OH-soh) lit:* skilful, learned; of great ability and with fine technique in any art (also used adjectivally)

Spanish*

Spanish terms have penetrated the English language far less than, for example, French. Here we list words derived from Spanish which are likely to occur in common usage, and military and sporting terms useful in more specialized contexts.

Pronunciation

a	long as in r*a*ther
c	as English *k* before consonants and *a, o* and *u,* and pronounced like *th* before *e* and *i*
d	as in English at the beginning of a word and pronounced *th* at the end of words and between vowels
e	may be long or short and the text should be followed
g	as in English before consonants and *a, o* and *u,* and pronounced gutturally before *e* and *i*
h	always silent
j	is guttural
ll	like *lli* in mi*lli*on in English
n	is long
q	pronounced *k* in que and qui
r	rolled when it begins a word or is preceded by *p, n,* or *s*
s	is soft
u	usually pronounced *oo,* but silent after *q*

*Some of the terms in this section (eg *chaparral, chicano, gaucho*) are Central and South American corruptions of original Spanish words.

A

a caballo   *(ah kah-BAH-lyoh)* on horseback

a cuento   *(ah KWEN-toh)* (payment) on account

afición   *(ah-fee-see-OHN)* enthusiasm, desire, longing (for), inclination (to)

aficionado   *(ah-fee-SEE-oh-NAH-doh) lit:* amateur; enthusiast, devotee

alcalde   *(al-KAL-day)* mayor, governor

alcázar   *(al-KAH-sar)* castle, fortification, palace, citadel; applied particularly to those built in Spain by the Moors

amigo   *(ah-MEE-goh)* friend

audiencia   *(ow-dee-ENS-ee-ya)* audience, formal interview; law court, court of justice

a vuestra salud   *(ah VWES-trah sah-LOOD)* to your health! cheers!

B

baile flamenco   *(BY-lay flah-MEN-koh) lit:* flamingo dance; flamenco dance, a traditional Spanish gypsy dance

bandarilla   *(bahn-dah-REEL-lyah)* dart with streamer thrust into the neck of the bull at a bullfight

barba a barba   *(BAR-bah ah BAR-bah) lit:* beard to beard; face to face

bolero *(boh-LAY-roh)* woman's short jacket (usually sleeveless); slow-moving dance, music for it; title of a well-known composition by Ravel written in this style

bracero *(brah-SEH-roh)* labourer, farmhand; Mexican labourer working in the United States

bronco *(BRAHN-koh) lit:* rough, coarse; wild or untamed horse

C

caballero *(kah-bah-LYER-oh)* cavalier, horseman, gentleman, knight, nobleman

cabaña *(kah-BAH-nyah)* hut, enclosure

camarero *(kah-mah-REH-roh)* waiter

camarilla *(kah-mah-REE-lyah)* cadre, clique, coterie

camino real *(kah-MEE-no ray-AL) lit:* royal road; highway, best means to a given end

cañada *(kah-NYAH-dah)* small canyon

cantina *(kahn-TEE-nah)* canteen, buffet, snack bar

capa y espada *(KAH-pah ee es-PAH-dah) lit:* cloak and dagger; clandestine, involving intrigue

casa *(KAH-sah)* house, residence, building

caudillo *(cow-DEE-lyoh)* captain, leader, chief; title of Francisco Franco (1892-1975), Commander-in-Chief of the Falangists in the Spanish Civil War, 1936-39, and Head of State, 1939-75

chaparral *(SHAP-ahr-rahl)* dense undergrowth

che/ché *(chay)* comrade, fellow, ally

chicano *(chee-KAH-noh)* person of Mexican

origin living in the United States

chile con carne *(CHEE-lay kon KAR-nay)* Mexican stew consisting of beef, onions, chilli powder and sometimes beans (anglicized to chilli con carne)

conquistador *(kohn-kees-tah-DOR) lit:* conqueror; Spanish conqueror of Mexico and Peru in the sixteenth century; (now used metaphorically to indicate) one who invades and exploits on a massive scale

contrabandista *(kohn-trah-bahn-DEES-tah)* smuggler, purveyor of illegal goods

corral *(koh-RAHL) lit:* farmyard; fenced area for cattle, horses, etc

corrida de toros *(koh-REE-dah day TOR-ohs)* bullfight

costa *(KOH-sta)* coast, coastline; shore; used to describe stretches of coast and their hinterlands (eg Costa Blanca, Costa Brava, Costa del Sol)

D

descamisados *(dehs-KAH-mee-SAH-dohs) lit:* shirtless ones; followers of Eva Peron (d 1952), the second wife of Juan Peron, President of Argentina (1946-55, 1973-74), and an active supporter of social reform

(el) diablo *(el DYAH-bloh)* (the) devil, fiend, demon

E

El Dorado *(el doh-RAH-doh) lit:* the gilded one; fictitious land or city of gold in South America

en casa *(en CAH-sah)* at home

escudo *(es-KOO-doh)* shield; courage

F

falange/Falange *(fah-LAHN-heh) lit:* phalanx; Spanish Fascist party, supporters of Francisco Franco

falangista *(fah-lahn-HEES-tah)* falangist; member of the Spanish Fascist party; supporter of Francisco Franco

fandango *(fan-DAN-goh)* very lively dance for two, music for it; nonsense, foolishness

fidelismo *(fee-del-EES-moh)* Castroism; followers of Fidel Castro (b 1927), who led the revolution against Batista in Cuba in 1959 and has led Cuba since that date, and his theory of Communism

G

gaucho *(GOW-choh)* mounted herdsman of American Indian extraction in the south of Latin America; full-fitting pant-skirt worn by cowboys

gracias *(GRAH-syahs)* many thanks, thank you

gringo *(GREEN-goh) lit:* foreign; any stranger in Mexico; (derogatory term for) foreigner, especially from North America

guano *(GWAH-no)* excrement of sea-birds used as a natural fertilizer (found and gathered particularly in Peru)

guerrilla *(geh-REE-lyah) lit:* small war; brush-fighting, warfare by irregulars

H

hacienda *(ah-SYEN-dah)* plantation, large estate with mansion

hasta la vista   *(AHS-tah lah VEES-tah)* see you later!

hasta luego   *(AHS-tah LWEH-goh)* (goodbye) until later!

hasta mañana   *(AHS-tah mah-NYAH-nah)* see you tomorrow!

hidalgo   *(ee-DAL-go) lit:* son of 'something'; gentleman by birth, nobleman

hombre   *(OHM-bray)* man

I

incomunicado   *(een-koh-mew-nee-KAH-doh)* isolated, cut off from all possible contact

J

junta   *(HOON-tah) lit:* council; group of military men or group with military support serving as an interim government

junto   *(HOON-toh)* cabal, political e ement seeking power

L

loco poco   *(LOH-coh POH-coh)* slightly crazy, a little mad

lo dicho, dicho   *(loh DEE-choh DEE-choh)* what is said, is said; things once said cannot be retracted

lo pasado, pasado   *(loh pah-SAH-doh pah-SAH-doh)* what is past, is past

M

machete   *(mah-SHAY-tay)* wide-bladed knife used to cut through heavy undergrowth

machismo   *(mah-KEES-moh)* (great emphasis upon)

masculinity or virility

major-domo *see* **mayordomo**

matador *(ma-tah-DOR) lit:* one who kills; bullfighter

mayordomo *(mah-yor-DOH-moh)* chief steward, head servant (in a household); anglicized as **major-domo**

mesa *(MEH-sah)* table, plateau

meseta *(meh-SAY-tah)* plain, plateau

mestizo *(mes-TEE-soh)* half-breed of mixed Indian and Spanish blood

mucho *(MOO-choh)* much

mudejar *(moo-DAY-har)* a Spanish Moor; architectural style showing a strong Moorish influence

N

novela picaresca *(noh-VEH-lah pee-kah-RES-kah)* picaresque novel, adventure story; book following the adventures of a single roguish hero

P

pacífico *(pah-SEE-fee-koh)* peaceful, pacific

padre *(PAH-dray)* father, priest

paella *(pah-ELL-yah)* Spanish dish containing rice, chicken, seafood, etc, cooked in a large shallow pan

pampas *(PAHM-pahs)* grassy plains of South America

paso doble *(PA-so DOH-blay) lit:* double step, quick march, quick-stepping dance

pecadillo *(peh-kah-DEE-lyoh)* minor transgression,

	venial offence (from pecado: sin)
peronista	*(peh-roh-NEES-tah)* follower of Juan Peron, President of Argentina 1946-55 and 1973-74
peso	*(PAY-soh)* weight; dollar
picador	*(pee-kah-DOR)* horseman who opens bullfight by provoking bull
pícaro	*(PEE-kah-roh)* rogue, rascal
pinto	*(PEEN-toh)* piebald horse
plaza de toros	*(PLAH-zah-day-TOH-rohs)* bullfighting ring
pochismo	*(poh-CHEES-moh)* pidgin Spanish/English spoken along Mexican/US border
politico	*(poh-LEE-tee-koh)* opportunist, advantage-seeker
poncho	*(POHN-choh)* two rectangular pieces of cloth sewn together to form cape fitting over head
premio gordo	*(PREH-mee-oh GOR-doh) lit:* fat prize; grand prize
pronto	*(PROHN-toh)* quickly, promptly
pueblo	*(PWEH-blo)* village, town; Indian reservation

Q

que será será	*(KAY seh-rah seh-rah)* what will be, will be (expression of resignation)

R

rodeo	*(roh-DAY-oh) lit:* rotating; round-up and horse show exhibiting riding and roping talents

S

salud y pesetas
(sah-LOOD ee peh-SAY-tahs) (may you enjoy) health and money

Santo Oficio
(SAHN-toh oh-FEE-see-oh) lit: the Holy Office; ecclesiastical tribunal for the suppression of heresy; (especially) the Inquisition into religious heresy in Spain c 1530-1700

savanna
(sah-VAN-nah) treeless plain or bushland in tropical and sub-tropical regions

señor
(seh-NYOR) Mr, sir, gentleman

señora
(seh-NYOR-ah) Mrs, madame, lady

señorita
(seh-nyor-EET-ah) Miss, young lady

siglo de oro
(SEE-gloh day OH-roh) the golden age, classical period; in Spain this spanned the sixteenth and early seventeenth centuries when Spain was dominant economically, culturally and militarily

sombrero
(sohm-BRAY-roh) hat with wide brim for shade

supremo
(soo-PRAY-moh) general, overlord, commander

T

tilde
(TEEL-dah) diacritical mark (~) over letter to indicate change of sound; *ñ* in Spanish should be pronounced *ny,* and *ã* and *õ* in Portuguese should be nasalized

toreador
(toh-ray-ah-DOR) bullfighter

toreo
(toh-RAY-oh) (art of) bullfighting

torero
(toh-RAY-roh) bullfighter, especially one responsible for killing the bull

toro   *(TOH-roh)* bull

V

vamoose   *(vah-MOOS)* beat it! go away!
(corruption of Spanish vamos: let us go)

vaquero   *(vah-KAY-roh)* herdsman; cowboy

vigilante   *(vee-gheel-AHN-tay) lit:* vigilance,
watchfulness; self-appointed champion
of law and order whose motive is often
revenge for a specific crime

Miscellaneous Languages

Words and phrases derived from a wide variety of languages have penetrated English. We have again included those which are used but not wholly integrated in the language and those which have particularly interesting derivations.

The phonetics should be followed to give a reasonably accurate rendering of the phrase, though the reader is advised to cross-check phrases using standard dictionaries in each language.

Key to abbreviations

Ar   Arabic

Aus   Australian

Ch   Chinese

Egyp Egyptian

Heb   Hebrew

Hd   Hindi

Ir   Irish

Jpn   Japanese

Pers Persian

Port Portuguese

Rus   Russian

Scot Scottish

Sk   Sanskrit

Turk Turkish

Yd   Yiddish

A

acushla *(Ir)*   *(ah-KOO-shla) lit:* pulse of my heart; my dearest (term of endearment)

aga/agha *(Turk)*   *(AH-ghah)* ruler, leader

ahimsa *(Sk)*   *(uh-HIM-suh) lit:* no injury; reverence for life, principle of non-violence

ankh *(Egyp)*   *(ahngh) lit:* life, soul; (Egyptian) cross symbolizing eternal life

aparthied
(Afrikaans)   *(uh-PAR-tayt)* the South African government's policy of racial segregation

apparat *(Rus)*   *(ap-PAR-aht) lit:* apparatus; structure of the Communist Party in the USSR; the collective term for the party functionaries who govern the USSR

apparatchik *(Rus)*   *(ap-PAR-aht-chik)* member of **apparat;** Communist party functionary

Ashkenazi *(Heb)*   *(osh-keh-NAH-zee)* Jew of Germany or Eastern Europe, usually Yiddish-speaking (*cf* **Sephardi**)

ataman *(Rus)*   *(uh-tuh-MAHN) lit:* head man; Cossack chief; elected leader of Cossacks

auto da fé *(Port)*   *(OW-toh da FEH) lit:* act of the faith; death (accepted) for a religious cause; (during the Inquisition) sentence of burning passed on heretics

avatar *(Sk)*   *(AH-vah-tahr)* incarnation of a deity; principle in concrete form; temporary state of being

B

babu *(Hd)*	*(BAH-boo) lit:* father; (in India) form of address similar to Mr, Sir, Esq; (pejorative term for) native, especially native clerk who writes in English
babushka *(Rus)*	*(BAH-boosh-kah) lit:* grandmother; headscarf tied under chin worn by peasant women
bagel *(Yd)*	*(BAY-g'l)* ring-shaped roll
bairn *(Scot)*	*(behrn)* child babe
baksheesh *(Pers)*	*(bahk-SHEESH)* tip, gratuity; buckshee is an alternati e English use
banzai *(Jap)*	*(bahn-ZY) lit:* (may you live for) 10,000 years; salute to the Japanese emperor; battle cry
bapuji *(Hd)*	*(BAH-poo-jee)* little father; term applied to Mahatma Ghandi
bar mitzvah *(Heb)*	*(bar MITS-vah) lit:* son of the commandment; ceremony for Jewish boys when they reach the age of thirteen and assume the religious duties of an adult
bhakti *(Sk)*	*(BHUK-tee)* religious devotion or worship
billabong *(Aus)*	*(BIL-uh-bong) lit:* dead river; backwater, stagnant pool in the bed of a stream
bolshevik *(Rus)*	*(BOL-shih-vik) lit:* one of the majority; those who followed Lenin, d 1924, after the SDWP split in 1903 (the greater number of those present at the party congress at which the division was crystallized followed Lenin); (former term for any) Russian communist
bolshoi *(Rus)*	*(bul-SHOY)* large, great; the **Bolshoi**

	ballet is one of the two finest Soviet ballet companies
borsch/borsht/ bortsch *(Rus)*	*(borsh/borsht/borshch)* soup made from beetroot and various other ingredients
braw *(Scot)*	*(brawr)* fine; good (especially of weather)
burra sahib *(Hd)*	*(BOO-rah sah-HEEB)* person of importance
bushido *(Jpn)*	*(BOO-shee-doh)* code of the **samurai**; code of honour adhered to by military knights
bwana *(Swahili)*	*(BWAH-nah) lit:* our father; master, form of address equivalent to Sir

C

cab(b)ala(h) *(Heb)*	*(ka-BAH-la)* Jewish mystical tradition; any esoteric or occult lore (also **kab(b)ala(h)**)
caftan *(Turk)*	*(KAHF-tahn)* long tunic secured by girdle at waist
casbah	*see* **kasbah**
Chas(s)id *(Heb)*	*(KHAH-sid)* member of a Jewish mystical movement which is characterized by simplicity and joyfulness *(plu:* **Chas(s)idim**) (also **Has(s)id**)
Chas(s)idim	*see* **Chas(s)id**
cheong-sam *(Ch)*	*(chay-OHNG-sahm)* long red dress worn by Chinese women on ceremonial occasions
chernozem *(Rus)*	*(CHAYR-noh-TSEHM) lit:* black earth; black soil of temperate and semi-arid areas such as parts of southern Russia
chi-chi *(Hd)*	*(CHEE-chee)* pidgin English spoken by Eurasians in India
chotchke	*see* **tchotchke**

chutzpah *(Yd)* — *(KHOOTZ-pah)* audacity, boldness, impudence

coolie *(Hd)* — *(COO-lee)* oriental labourer (especially in South Africa); derogatory term for Indian worker

czar — *see* **tsar**

czarevitch — *see* **tsarevitch**

czarevna — *see* **tsarevna**

czarina — *see* **tsarina**

D

Dalai Lama *(Mongolian)* — *(DAH-ly LAH-mah)* title of Tibetan priest-king (overthrown in 1959)

ding hao *(Ch)* — *(DING how)* very good, fine, excellent

djibbah *(Ar)* — *(JUH-bah)* long-sleeved coat worn by Muslims

dreck *(Yd)* — *(drek)* filth, rubbish, excrement

Duma *(Rus)* — *(DOO-muh)* Russian parliament (1905-17); council to Nicholas II

dybbuk *(Heb)* — *(DIB-book)* evil spirit; soul of a dead person which enters a living body

E

effendi *(Turk)* — *(eh-FEN-dee)* master; title of respect used to address superior

eisteddfod *(Welsh)* — *(ay-STETH-vohd)* lit: session; musical or poetic contest(s) at national or local level

emir *(Ar)* — *(eh-MEER)* commander, leader, governor

F

fakir *(Ar)* — *(fah-KEER)* lit: poor man; Muslim or

Hindu ascetic

fan-tan *(Ch)* *(fahn-tahn)* card game in which players attempt to dispose of seven cards before their opponents

fellah *(Ar)* *(fel-LAH)* Egyptian peasant (*plu:* **fellahin**)

fellahin *see* **fellah**

fidalgo *(Port)* *(fee-DAHL-goh)* gentleman, noble; *see* **hidalgo**

G

geisha *(Jpn)* *(GAY-shah)* professional female dancer and entertainer; companion for men in Japan

gomei kaisha *(Jpn)* *(GOH-may KY-shah)* partnership, association

goy *(Yd)* *(goy) lit:* people, nation; term (often derogatory) used by a Jew to refer to a non-Jew

gung-ho *(Ch)* *(gung-hoh) lit:* work together; (excessively) loyal or enthusiastic

guru *(Hd)* *(GOO-roo)* teacher, mentor; spiritual leader

H

hara kiri *(Jpn)* *(HAH-rah KEE-ree) lit:* stomach-cutting; ceremonial suicide by disembowelment

Has(s)id *see* **Chas(s)id**

I

imam *(Ar)* *(ee-MAHM)* Muslim priest; leader of congregation prayer in a mosque; religious leader of the Shiites regarded as divinely inspired

J

jihad *(Ar)*   *(jee-HAHD) lit:* conflict; crusade, holy war undertaken by Muslims against infidels

jinrickshaw *(Jpn)*   *(jihn-RIK-shah)* two-wheeled cab pulled by one or more persons

K

ka *(Egyp)*   *(kah)* soul, spirit, life force

kab(b)ala(h)   *see* **cab(b)ala(h)**

Kaddish *(Aramaic)*   *(Kah-dish)* doxology recited as the last synagogue prayer, and at the grave in memory of the dead

kaffir *(Ar)*   *(KAH-feer)* infidel, (Muslim) heretic; derogatory term for Black African

kamikaze *(Jpn)*   *(KAH-mee-KAH-zeh) lit:* divine wind; (in World War II) Japanese pilot(s) who crashed aircraft filled with explosives into enemy ships; any suicide mission (usually used adjectivally in English)

karma *(Sk)*   *(KAR-muh)* the sum of an individual life; fate, destiny, (retributive) justice at the end of a person's life

kasbah *(Ar)*   *(KAHS-bah)* Arab quarter of a North African city; the old part of a city, marked by a citadel (also **casbah**)

katana *(Jpn)*   *(KAH-tah-nah)* sword used by **samurai**

kayak *(Eskimo)*   *(KY-ahk)* Eskimo canoe of sealskin stretched over light frame fitted to canoeist's waist

khushi *(Hd)*   *(KOO-shee)* pleasure, happiness, contentment

kibbutz *(Heb)*   *(keeb-BOOTZ) lit:* gathering; cooperative settlement; agricultural collective

kibitzer *(Yd)*   *(KIB-itz-er)* meddler, busybody, back-seat driver

kimono *(Jpn)*   *(kee-MO-noh)* woman's robe which is long, has wide sleeves and is tied with a sash

kismet *(Turk)*   *(KIS-meht)* fate, destiny, the will of Allah

kiwi *(Maori)*   *(KEE-wee)* New Zealand bird incapable of flight; New Zealander

kolkhoz *(Rus)*   *(kul-KOHS)* collective farm in USSR

Kol Nidre *(Aramaic)*   *(kohl NEE-dreh)* prayer of atonement offered on the eve of Yom Kippur

kosher *(Yd)*   *(KOH-shur) lit:* right, proper; ritually clean; in compliance with Jewish dietary laws; pious; legitimate; reliable

kowtow *(Ch)*   *(KOW-tow)* obsequious behaviour, fawning, bowing low

kulak *(Rus)*   *(koo-LAK) lit:* tight-fisted person; landowner with small amount of property in Russia immediately prior to the 1917 revolution; propertied class encouraged by the government of Nicholas II as a bolster against possible revolution and subject to vigorous attack after the revolution, particularly in the period of collectivization under Stalin in the late 1920s

kung fu *(Ch)*   *(koung foo)* Chinese martial art combining the disciplines of karate and judo

kvetch *(Yd)*   *(kvetch)* to complain, gripe

L

lama *(Tibetan)* — *(LAH-meh)* (in Tibet) Buddhist priest or monk

leprechaun *(Ir)* — *(LEH-preh-kahn)* small body; diminutive sprite; impish creature of legend who repays kindness

M

maelstrom *(Dutch)* — *(MAHL-strom)* whirlpool; irresistible force

malik *(Ar)* — *(MAH-leek)* chief, leader

mana *(Maori)* — *(MAH-nah)* charisma, charm, supernatural attraction

matzo(h) *(Yd)* — *(MOTT-seh)* unleavened bread, eaten especially during Passover

mazel tov *(Heb/Yd)* — *(MAH-zehl tohv)* congratulations!

memsahib *(Anglo-Indian)* — *(MEM-sah-heeb)* European lady; term of address equivalent to Madame

mensch *(Yd)* — *(mensh)* admirable, honourable person

menshevik *(Rus)* — *(MEN-shih-vik) lit:* the minority; term describing those who followed George Plekhanov after the SDWP split in 1903

meshuggah/ meshugge *(Yd)* — *(me-SHU-geh) lit:* crazy; insane, deranged

mezuzah *(Heb)* — *(me-ZU-zah)* small oblong case containing verses from Deuteronomy inscribed on parchment, affixed to doorpost of a Jewish home

mikado *(Jpn)* — *(mee-KAH-doh)* (title of) emperor of Japan

minyan *(Heb)* — *(MIN-yon) lit:* number; quorum of ten

men necessary for Jewish religious services

mufti *(Ar)* — *(MOOF-tee) lit:* arbiter; teacher, adviser; Muslim expert in the laws of the Koran; non-uniform dress

mullah *(Ar)* — *(moo-LAH) lit:* master; Muslim religious teacher, scholar, leader

N

nabob *(Hd)* — *(NAY-bahb)* personage of power and wealth; man who acquired wealth and status through service or commerce in India in the late eighteenth and nineteenth centuries (corruption of **nawab**)

nawab *(Hd)* — *(nuh-WAWB)* governor, Indian prince

nebbish/nebech *(Yd)* — *(NEB-ish)* unlucky, timid, insignificant person

nirvana *(Sk)* — *(neer-VAH-nah) lit:* extinction; perfect state; the negation of personal desire and need as ultimate reward for holiness; absorption into Brahman achieved by extinguishing individual identity and egoism

.osn *(Yd)* — *(nosh) n:* snack or meal; *v:* to eat a snack or meal

nu *(Yd)* — *(noo)* versatile interjection expressing any number of emotions: well?; so?; what's new?; etc

nudnik *(Yd)* — *(NOOD-nik)* a bore; a pest

O

oblast *(Rus)* — *(OH-bluhst)* province or district in the USSR

okimono *(Jpn)* — *(OH-kee-moh-noh)* decorative objects

omadhaun *(Ir)*   *(oh-MA WD-hahn)* madman, lunatic

ombudsman *(Swedish)*   *(OHM-buds-man) lit:* legal representative; (in the UK) the official to whom complaints against government authorities are sent to be investigated

origami *(Jpn)*   *(OH-ree-gah-mee)* art of folding paper into intricate patterns and models

oy/oy vay *(Yd)*   *(oy VAY)* ejaculation expressing surprise, horror, pain, despair, etc, as well as delight or relief

P

pagoda *(Port)*   *(pah-GOH-dah)* tower of several stories; temple in India or the Far East

pariah *(Hd)*   *(puh-RY-uh) lit:* drummer; outcast; (formerly) member of low caste or of no caste in southern India

pasha *(Turk)*   *(PAH-shah)* high official in former Turkish empire

pundit *(Hd)*   *(PUHN-dit)* (formerly) scholar, person who speaks with authority regarding a wide variety of subjects; has derogatory overtones in English, suggesting a professional but not necessarily scholarly or discriminating commentator

purdah *(Hd)*   *(PUR-dah) lit:* veil; cloth concealing the face of women in Hindu and Muslim communities; discriminatory practices including the absolute seclusion of women in Oriental countries

Q

quisling *(Norwegian)*   *(KWIZ-ling)* collaborator, traitor; after Vidkun Quisling, a Norwegian army officer who supported the Nazis after

their occupation of Norway during
World War II

R

raj *(Hd)* — *(rahj)* authority, rule; particularly British Imperial rule in India

rajah *(Hd)* — *(RAHJ-ah) lit:* ruler; Indian prince; (in Malaya and Java) ruler, chieftain

S

sahib *(Hd)* — *(SAH-heeb) lit:* friend, lord; form of address used by Indians when speaking of or to Europeans

salaam *(Ar)* — *(sah-LAHM)* peace (be with you); salutation of low bow with right palm on forehead

samizdat *(Rus)* — *(suh-MEEZ-daht)* system of printing and distributing illegal and dissident literature in the USSR

samovar *(Rus)* — *(sah-moh-VAR) lit:* self-boiler; tea-making apparatus with interior heating to keep water at boiling point

sampan *(Ch)* — *(SAHM-pan)* simple ship propelled by oars or a single sail

samurai *(Jpn)* — *(SAH-moo-ry)* warrior caste of feudal Japan; militant aristocracy which was the administrative and military base of Japan from the eleventh to the nineteenth centuries

sari *(Hd)* — *(SAH-ree)* dress worn by women in India

sarong *(Malaysian)* — *(SAH-rohng)* skirt or draped dress worn in the South Pacific

sati — *see* **suttee**

satyagraha *(Sk)*	*(sut-yah-GRUH-huh) lit:* grasping truth; policy of passive resistance to British rule initiated by Gandhi in the 1920s; any movement of non-violent resistance
schlemiel	*see* **shlemiel**
schlep	*see* **shlep**
schlimazel	*see* **shlimazl**
schlok	*see* **shlock**
schmaltz	*see* **shmaltz**
schmuck	*see* **shmuck**
schnook	*see* **shnook**
schnorrer	*see* **shnorrer**
Seder *(Heb)*	*(SAY-dur)* ceremonial feast held on the evenings preceding the first and second days of Passover
Sephardi *(Heb)*	*(seh-FAR-dee)* Jew of Spanish or Portuguese descent (*cf* **Ashkenazi**)
sepoy *(Hd)*	*(SEE-poy)* (formerly) native Indian soldier under British command
shalom *(Heb)*	*(shah-LOHM) lit:* peace; salutation at meeting or parting
sheikh *(Ar)*	*(shaykh)* chief, tribal head
shekel *(Heb)*	*(SHEK'l)* coin; money
shiksa *(Yd)*	*(SHIK-sa)* non-Jewish woman
shillelagh *(Ir)*	*(shuh-LAY-lee)* heavy walking stick; stout club, cudgel; from Shillelagh, the town in County Wicklow, Ireland, which first produced such cudgels
shlemiel *(Yd)*	*(shleh-MEEL)* fool; unlucky or clumsy person (also **schlemiel**)
shlep *(Yd)*	*(shlep) v:* to drag; *n:* tedious or unlucky person (also **schlep**)

shlimazl *(Yd)*   *(shlih-MAZ-z'l)* unlucky person (also **schlimazel**)

shlock *(Yd)*   *(shlohk)* cheap, inferior item (also **schlok**)

shmaltz *(Yd)*   *(shmahltz)* cooking (usually chicken) fat; excessive sentimentality (also **schmaltz**)

shmatte *(Yd)*   *(SHMAH-ta)* rag, cheap piece of clothing; person unworthy of respect

shmeer *(Yd)*   *(shmeer)* smear; bribe; paint

shmuck *(Yd)*   *(shmuck)* penis; stupid or detestable person (also **schmuck**)

schnook *(Yd/American)*   *(shnook)* a pitiable or timid person (also **schnook**)

shnorrer *(Yd)*   *(SHNOHR-er)* beggar; idler; bargain-hunter (also **schnorrer**)

shtetl *(Yd)*   *(SHTEH-t'l)* Jewish community in Eastern Europe before World War II

shtik *(Yd)*   *(shtik)* piece, part; contrived bit of acting

shul *(Yd)*   *(shool)* synagogue

simoom *(Ar)*   *(SEE-moom)* hot, dry desert wind

skal *(Norwegian)*   *(skohl)* to your health!

springbok *(Afrikaans)*   *(SPRING-bohk)* gazelle indigenous to South Africa

steppe *(Rus)*   *(stehp) lit:* lowland; flat, treeless plain

(de) Stijl *(Dutch)*   *(de STYL) lit:* the style; group of architects and artists, including Mondrian and van Doesburg, in the Netherlands in the 1920s devoted to neoplasticism and, later, Dadaism; the magazine published by this group

sutra *(Hd)*   *(SOO-tra)* set of tenets in Hindu teaching; the narrative of the teachings of Buddha

suttee *(Hd)*	*(SUHT-ee)* custom of Hindi widows burning themselves on their husbands' funeral pyres; also termed **sati**: faithful wife
swami *(Hd)*	*(SWAH-mee)* Hindu religious leader
swastika *(Hd)*	*(SWUH-stee-KUH)* *lit:* prosperity, well-being; ancient religious symbol in the shape of a Greek cross, adopted by the Nazis in 1935 as the emblem of Nazi Germany

T

taboo *(Polynesian)*	*(tah-BOO)* sacred, prohibited, also used as a noun in English
Talmud *(Heb)*	*(TAHL-mood)* collection of Jewish law and tradition; it consists of the Mishna and the Gemara
tamasha *(Hd)*	*(tahm-MA-shah)* entertainment or public function; commotion, fuss
tantra *(Sk)*	*(TAHN-trah)* *lit:* doctrine; (type of) mystical Buddhist work
Tao *(Ch)*	*(TOW)* *lit:* pathway; the right way, the rational basis of human conduct; cosmic order
tchotchke *(Yd)*	*(TCHOTCH-keh)* knick-knack; toy; attractive woman; unimportant person (also **chotchke, tsatske**)
tepee *(American Indian)*	*(TEE-pee)* tent, wigwam
tong *(Ch)*	*(tahng)* *lit:* meeting place; secret organization (usually involved in clandestine activities)
Torah *(Heb)*	*(TOW-ra)* the Pentateuch; scroll containing this; all Jewish law, teachings, tradition

totem *(American Indian)*   *(TOH-tehm)* hereditary emblem of tribe or individual which is held sacred; usually an animal or creature of the earth or sky

troika *(Rus)*   *(TROY-kuh)* three-horse cart; used metaphorically to indicate three ideas or three aspects of one idea

tsar *(Rus)*   *(tsahr)* title of male Russian rulers who governed before the revolution of 1917 (also **czar**)

tsarevitch *(Rus)*   *(TSAH-reh-vich)* son of the **tsar** or **tsarina**; heir apparent to the throne (also **czarevitch**)

tsarevna *(Rus)*   *(tsah-REV-nuh)* daughter of the **tsar** (also **czarevna**)

tsarina *(Rus)*   *(tsah-REE-nuh)* Russian empress (also **czarina**)

tsatske   *see* **tchotchke**

U

uhuru *(Swahili)*   *(oo-HOO-roo)* freedom, liberation; national independence (particularly) in East Africa

V

veld *(Afrikaans)*   *(felt)* *lit:* field; uncultivated bushland or scrubland

verkrampte *(Afrikaans)*   *(fer-KRAMP-teh)* (South African) considered reactionary and pro-apartheid

verligte *(Afrikaans)*   *(fer-LIG-teh)* (South African considered) relatively liberal and enlightened

voodoo *(Haitian)*   *(VOO-doo)* magical rituals associated with religious beliefs

W

wen *(Ch)*
(WUN) literature, letters, culture

wigwam *(American Indian)*
(WIG-wahm) hut, lodge or tent used as dwelling

Y

yarmulke *(Yd)*
(YAR-m'l-kuh) man's skullcap worn by Jews at prayer, and by religious Jews at all times

yashmak *(Turk)*
(yahsh-MAHK) veil worn by Muslim women

yenta *(Yd)*
(YEN-ta) shrewish woman; a gossip

yeshiva *(Heb)*
(yeh-SHEE-va) Orthodox Jewish school

yoga *(Hd)*
(YOH-gah) lit: union; Hindu philosophy that aims at a union of the self with the supreme being through a set of mental and physical exercises

yogi *(Hd)*
(YOH-gee) one who teaches **yoga**

Z

zen *(Jpn)*
(zen) form of Buddhism emphasizing meditation and introspection as the means of achieving enlightenment and fulfilment

Appendix 1:
Words derived from Classical History and Mythology

A

academy *(Gk)* — place of learning; from the grove of Academos outside Athens, where Plato taught

Achilles' heel *(Gk)* — weak spot, point vulnerable to attack; in Homer's *Iliad*, Achilles was protected at every point except his heel, into which Paris shot an arrow and killed him

actaeon *(Gk)* — cuckold, one with horns implanted upon him; Actaeon was a hunter who one day discovered Artemis bathing. Offended, she turned him into a stag and he was killed by his own hounds

adonis *(Gk)* — handsome young man; Adonis was a beautiful youth, beloved of Aphrodite and killed by a wild boar

aegis *(Gk)* — protection, patronage, auspices; under the **aegis** of: to be protected by; the aegis was the shield of Zeus, covered with the skin of the goat, Amalthea

aeolian *(Gk)* — borne on the wind; from Aiolos (*Lat:* Aeolus), god of the winds

agonippe *(Gk)* — poetic inspiration; Agonippe was a fountain on Mount Helicon, sacred to the Muses

amazon *(Gk)* — female soldier; warlike, manlike, strong or vigorous woman; the Amazons were a nation of single-breasted female warriors located in Asia or Scythia

ambrosia *(Gk)* — something sweet or pleasing; ambrosia was the food of the Greek gods and conferred everlasting youth and beauty

aphrodisiac *(Gk)* — a sexual stimulant; from Aphrodite the goddess of love

apollo *(Gk)* — man of great beauty; Apollo was the sun god

arcadia *(Gk)* — paradise, place of great beauty and pastoral simplicity; Arkadia was a mountain district in the Peloponnese, regarded as the epitome of rural bliss and serenity

atlas *(Gk)* — man renowned for physical strength; from the Titan condemned to support the heavens on his shoulders for rebelling against Zeus. The name is given to a collection of maps because the figure of Atlas was used to decorate the title page of Mercator's collection in 1595

aurora *(Gk)* — lights in the northern and southern night sky; Aurora was the goddess of the dawn

B

bacchic/ bacchanalian *(Lat)* — riotous, tending to indulge in drunken revelry; Bacchus was the god of wine, and Bacchanalia was the festival devoted to him

boreal *(Gk)* — northern, of the north; from Boreas, the north wind

C

cadmean/ cadmeian *(Gk)* — victory gained at too great cost; victory so costly in terms of losses that it is barely worth winning; Cadmus sowed dragon's teeth, from which sprang soldiers who fought each other until only five were left; *see* **pyrrhic**

cassandra *(Gk)* (one who makes) an unheeded prophecy; Cassandra, the priestess and daughter of Priam, King of Troy, was gifted with prophecy but doomed never to be believed

chimerical *(Gk)* wildly fanciful; the Chimera was a fabulous monster with a lion's head, goat's body and serpent's tail slain by Bellerophon while he was riding the flying horse Pegasus

colossal *(Gk)* gigantic, huge, splendid; a colossus was a gigantic human statue, the most famous of these, the Colossus of Rhodes, was one of the seven wonders of the ancient world

D

daedalian/ daedalean *(Gk)* intricate, displaying great invention and artistic skill and complexity; Daedalus built the Cretan labyrinth

damoclean *(Gk)* (situation of) imminent danger. Sword of Damocles: imminent danger, immediate threat; Damocles feasted with a sword suspended by a single hair hanging over him

delphic *(Gk)* ambiguous, enigmatic; Delphi was the site of a famous oracle of Apollo, whose answers tended to be double-edged

demosthenic *(Gk)* eloquent, articulate and powerful speaker; like Demosthenes or his oratory; Demosthenes was an Athenian statesman and orator, and a powerful opponent of Macedonian power over Greece

draconian *(Gk)* harsh, severe, rigorous; from Draco the seventh century BC Athenian lawgiver, who demanded the death penalty for almost every infringement of his code

E

egeria *(Lat)*   female adviser, patroness; Egeria was the nymph who was reputed to have given Numa Pompilius, second king of Rome the laws for which he was famed

epicurean *(Gk)*   one preferring sensual pleasures, hedonist, follower of Epicurus; Epicurus was a Greek philosopher who taught that fulfilment lay in self-satisfaction and the absence of fear (*cf* **stoic**)

erebus *(Gk)*   terrifying and isolated spot; Erebus was a place of darkness between earth and Hades

erotic *(Gk)*   producing sexual passion; from Eros the Greek god of love

F

furies *(Gk)*   avenging spirits, remorseful pangs; the Furies were snake-haired goddesses — Alecto, Tisiphone and Megaera — sent from Tartarus to punish people who committed crimes

G

ganymedes *(Gk)*   waiter, potboy; Ganymedes was the cupbearer of Zeus

gordian *(Gk)*   Gordian knot: complex problem, difficult task; to cut the Gordian knot: sidestep the complexities by taking more forthright action; Gordius tied the knot cut by Alexander the Great

H

hebe *(Gk)*   waitress, barmaid; Hebe was goddess of youth, daughter of Zeus and Hera, and cupbearer of Olympus

heliconian *(Gk)*   inspirational, uplifting; Helicon was a mountain sacred to the Muses

herculean *(Lat)*   strong as Hercules, of prodigious strength; Hercules *(Gk: Herakles)* carried out twelve immense tasks

hippocratic *(Gk)*   the hippocratic oath is signed by those beginning the practice of medicine and expresses a commitment to ethical conduct; Hippocrates was a physician in Greece in the fifth century BC

hydra *(Gk)*   something which is difficult to extinguish; the Hydra was a serpent whose heads multiplied as they were cut off

hyperborean *(Gk)*   *lit:* beyond the north wind; inhabitant of the north (of a land), something from the far north; the Greeks believed that a people of this name lived, each to the age of 1000 years, in peace and happiness under cloudless skies somewhere beyond the north wind

I

iliad *(Gk)*   long series; the *Iliad* is an epic poem written by Homer culminating in the description of the siege of Troy

L

laconic *(Gk)*   brief, terse, concise; Laconia, another term for Sparta, was noted for the austerity of its customs

lethean *(Gk)*   forgetful, unable to recollect past events; Lethe was a river in Hades that produced amnesia in those who travelled along it

lotus *(Gk)*	^lotus eater: person given to indulgence and indolence; from lotos, a plant supposed to produce indolence and sloth
lyceum *(Gk)*	lecture hall, teaching place, literary institution; the Lyceum was the school and playing field in Athens where Aristotle taught

M

marathon *(Gk)*	a race of great length; requiring extreme endurance (applied to competitions of all kinds); Pheidippides is reputed to have run 150 miles to secure spartan aid for the Athenians at the battle of Marathon in 490 BC
martial *(Lat)*	related to warfare; from Mars, the god of war
medusa *(Gk)*	hideous woman, someone impossible to look at without revulsion; Medusa was a woman turned into a gorgon by Athena and, if looked at directly, turned her beholder to stone
mentor *(Gk)*	wise counsellor, trusted adviser; Mentor was advisor to Telemachus in Homer's *Odyssey*
mercurial *(Lat)*	volatile, changeable, quick-witted; from Mercury (*Gk:* **Hermes**), the swift-footed messenger of the Gods
midas *(Gk)*	Midas touch: ability to make money in any activity; Midas was a mythical king of Phrygia, whose touch turned all objects to gold
morphine *(Gk)*	drug extracted from opium which reduces pain and induces sleep; from Morpheus, the god of dreams
muse *(Gk)*	(goddess) inspiring a creative artist; the

Muses were nine sister goddesses each responsible for a separate art

myrmidon *(Gk)*   a brigand under a fearless leader; one who boldly executes another's orders; the Myrmidons were a tribe of warriors led by Achilles in the attack on Troy

N

narcissism *(Gk)*   excessive self-love, great vanity, obsession with one's own personal perfection; Narcissus was a beautiful youth who fell in love with his own reflection in a pool, refused to leave the water's edge and died, and was turned into the flower which bears his name

nectar *(Gk)*   delicious drink, sweet beverage, nectar was the drink of the gods

nemesis *(Gk)*   retribution, personification of divine wrath; Nemesis was the goddess of vengeance

nestor *(Gk)*   old man; aged counsellor; Nestor was represented in Homer's *Iliad* as the oldest and wisest Greek in the Trojan war

niobe *(Gk)*   bereaved woman who cannot be consoled; Niobe, a daughter of Tantalus, could not stop weeping, for nine days and nights, for her 14 slain children and continued to weep even after she had been turned to stone

O

odyssey *(Gk)*   a long journey; story of a long journey; relating to the *Odyssey*, an epic poem attributed to Homer describing the return of the Greeks from the Trojan war and especially concerned with Odysseus

oedipus *(Gk)* — one who solves riddles; Oedipus solved the Sphinx's riddle; he was the son of Laius and Jocasta and, unaware of his parentage, killed his father and married his mother. Hence Oedipus complex: the name given to Freud's theory that a male child is sexually attracted to his mother and jealous of his father

olympiad *(Gk)* — a period of four years, which is the interval between celebrating the Olympic Games; also the celebration of the Olympic Games; regular international competition in chess, etc; Olympia was a plain in north west Peloponnese and a sanctuary of Zeus where the sporting and artistic competitions which formed the first Olympic Games were held

olympian *(Gk)* — grand, magnificent, celestial; superior and detached; Olympus was the Thessalian mountain on which the classical Greek gods dwelt

orphic/orphean *(Gk)* — mysterious, oracular, mystical; of Orpheus and the mysteries associated with nim; Orpheus, the Greek poet and musician charmed the gods of the underworld by his singing into restoring his dead wife Eurydice to life on earth on condition that he did not look at her until he reached the upper world; he did so, she was lost and he was later torn to pieces by Thracian women during an orgy in honour of Dionysos. The Orphic Cult was a religious movement with secret rites thought to be concerned with fertility rituals

oxygian *(Gk)* — prehistoric, of obscure origin; Oxygios was a mythical king of Attica or Boetia

P

palladium *(Gk)* (source of) security, something on which an institution is dependent; from the image of Pallas which was originally sent down by Zeus to Dardanus, founder of Troy, and on the safety of which depended the fate of Troy; hence anything on which the safety of an individual or people depends

Pandora's box *(Gk)* source of great and unexpected troubles; Pandora was the first woman on earth who, by disregarding the order not to open the box she had been given, she released all the troubles and sins which beset human beings

platonic *(Gk)* relating to the ideas of Plato; relating to ideas generally, rather than action; platonic love: spiritual relationship, ie one without a sexual dimension; Plato, d 347 BC, was a pupil of Socrates and author of the *Dialogues*, which encapsulated much of Socrates' thinking

priapism *(Gk)* licentiousness, promiscuity; Priapus was the god of procreation

protean *(Gk)* thing or person readily assuming different shapes; Proteus was a sea-god who assumed many different shapes to evade having to foretell the future

pyrrhic *(Lat)* (victory) gained at too high a cost; from Pyrrhus, king of Epirus, who defeated the Romans at Asculeum in 279 BC, but was as much weakened in victory as his enemy in defeat; *see* **cadmean**

R

rhadamanthine *(Gk)* unbending and incorruptible;

Rhadamanthus was the severe judge who presided over the court of the underworld

S

sapphism *(Gk)*

lesbianism; Sappho was a lyric poetess in Lesbos in the sixth century BC who is believed to have been a lesbian

saturnalia *(Lat)*

wild revelry, uproarious merrymaking; the uproarious Roman New Year festivities when, like the Lords of Misrule during the old Twelve Days of Christmas, the servants became the masters and the masters the servants

saturnine *(Lat)*

gloomy, melancholic; from Saturn, the father of Jupiter

satyr *(Gk)*

man of great sexual appetite; satyrs were sylvan deities, goat-like men who followed Dionysus in his debaucheries

Scylla and Charybdis *(Gk)*

a dual danger, in which the avoidance of one necessitates facing the second, in a predicament; in Homer's *Odyssey*, Scylla was a six headed monster who lived in a cave. If a ship came near enough, she would seize and devour the sailors, six at a time, and Charybdis was a whirlpool adjacent to it in the Straits of Messina; avoiding one put one in danger of being destroyed by the other

sibyl *(Gk)*

old fortune-teller, soothsayer, sorceress, hag; sibyls were women who in ancient times acted at various places — Cumae, Erythra, etc — as a mouthpiece of some god, and to whom many collections of oracles and prophecies were attributed

siren *(Gk)*

alluring or seductive woman; the sirens were sea-nymphs whose singing lured sailors on to rocks where they perished

socratic *(Gk)*

pertaining to Socrates, Socratic irony: pose of ignorance with the intention of exposing the ignorance of others; Socratic method: technique of teaching and discussion by means of question and answer, in which Socrates questioned the basic premises or assumptions of his students' arguments; Socrates, d 399 BC, was an Athenian philosopher, none of whose writing has survived but whose views and methods are reflected in the works of Plato and Xenophon

spartan *(Gk)*

austere, simplistic, enduring; Sparta was a Greek city in the south Peloponnese whose citizens were noted for their austerity and military prowess; *see* **laconic**

stoic *(Gk)*

(person with) self control and austere manners; the Stoics, founded in Athens by Zeno in 308 BC, believed that men could only be fulfilled by simple living and submission to fate (*cf* **Epicurean**)

stygian *(Gk)*

murky, gloomy, pertaining to the river Styx; the Styx was one of the rivers of Hades

sybaritic *(Gk)*

luxuriant, effeminate; the south Italian Greek colony, Sybaris, was renowned for its luxury

T

tantalus *(Gk)*

something which can be seen but not obtained; Tantalus, the son of Zeus, was condemned in Tartarus to stand in water that receded when he attempted to drink it and under fruit that moved away when he tried to touch it

terpsichorean *(Gk)*

relating to dancing; Terpsichore was the Muse of dancing and choral song

themis *(Gk)*   the personification of justice; Themis was the goddess of law and justice

thespian *(Gk)*   relating to Thespis; relating to drama and acting; Thespis is thought to have developed the dramatic form in the sixth century BC by the introduction of an actor who conversed with the chorus leader

titan *(Gk)*   person of superhuman size and strength; the Titans were the 12 children of Gaea (the earth god) and Uranus (the sky god). At their mother's instigation, they overthrew Uranus and set up Kronos in his place. When Zeus overthrew Kronos the titans rallied to their father's support, but Zeus and the other Olympians defeated them and confined them, all except Atlas and Prometheus, to Tartarus — an abyss below Hades

trojan *(Gk)*   somebody of great courage and tenacity; the Trojans defended their city of Troy with great determination for 10 years against the Greeks led by Agamemnon

trojan horse *(Gk)*   a trap to defeat an enemy; during the siege of Troy the Greeks feigned retreat and left behind a wooden horse — the Trojan horse — containing Greek soldiers. The Trojans brought it into the city and the Greeks within it launched a surprise attack, opened the gates of Troy, and thereby ensured a Greek victory

typhoon *(Gk)*   wind of hurricane force; from Typhon a hundred-headed giant killed by Zeus

Z

zephyr *(Gk)*   gentle breeze; soft fabric; zephyros was the god of the west wind

Appendix 2:
Greek and Latin Prefixes

a — *(Gk)* not

a —, **abs** — *(Lat)* from

ac — *(Lat)* to(wards)

acantho — *(Gk)* spiny, thorny

acous — *(Gk)* hearing

acro — *(Gk)* top, tip

actino — *(Gk)* ray (of light)

ad — *(Lat)* to(wards)

adeno — *(Gk)* gland

aero — *(Gk)* gas, air

af —, **ag** —, **al** — *(Lat)* to(wards)

allo — *(Gk)* other

alti —, **alto** — *(Lat)* high

ambi — *(Lat)* both

amphi — *(Gk)* both, around

amylo — *(Gk)* starch

an — *(Gk)* not

an — *(Lat)* to(wards)

ana — *(Gk)* again, thorough(ly)

andro — *(Gk)* man

anemo — *(Gk)* wind

ankylo — *(Gk)* curved, bent

ante — *(Lat)* before

anthropo — *(Gk)* man

anti — *(Gk)* against

ap — *(Lat)* to(wards)

api — *(Lat)* bee

apo — *(Gk)* away

aqui — *(Lat)* water

arbori — *(Lat)* tree

archaeo — *(Gk)* ancient, old

arch(i) — *(Gk)* chief

arthro — *(Gk)* joint

as — *(Lat)* to(wards)

aster —, **astro** — *(Gk)* star

at — *(Lat)* to(wards)

atmo — *(Gk)* vapour

audio — *(Lat)* hearing

auto — *(Gk)* self

avi — *(Lat)* bird

azo — *(Gk)* nitrogen

bacci — *(Lat)* berry

baro — *(Gk)* weight, heaviness

batho —, **bathy** — *(Gk)* deep

biblio — *(Gk)* book

bio — *(Gk)* life

blasto — *(Gk)* bud

blepharo — *(Gk)* eyelid

bracchio — *(Gk)* arm

brachy — *(Gk)* short

brady — *(Gk)* slow

branchio — *(Gk)* gills

brevi — *(Lat)* short

broncho — *(Gk)* throat

caco — *(Gk)* evil, bad

calci — *(Lat)* lime (mineral)

cardio — *(Gk)* heart

carpo — *(Gk)* fruit

cath —, cato — *(Gk)* down, thorough(ly)

ceno — *(Gk)* common

centi — *(Lat)* hundred

cephalo — *(Gk)* head

cerebro — *(Lat)* brain

cero — *(Gk)* wax

cervico — *(Lat)* neck

chalco — *(Gk)* bronze, copper

chilo — *(Gk)* lip

chiro — *(Gk)* hand

chloro — *(Gk)* green

chole —, cholo — *(Gk)* bile

chondro — *(Gk)* cartilage

choreo — *(Gk)* dance

choro — *(Gk)* country

chrom(at)o — *(Gk)* colour

chrono — *(Gk)* time

chryso — *(Gk)* gold

circum — *(Lat)* around

cirro — *(Lat)* curl

cis — *(Lat)* near to, on the near side of

cleisto — *(Gk)* closed

clino — *(Gk)* slope

co — *(Lat)* thorough(ly), with

cocci — *(Gk)* berry-shaped

coela — *(Gk)* stomach

com —, con —, col — *(Lat)* thorough(ly), with

conio — *(Gk)* dust

contra — *(Lat)* against

copro — *(Gk)* excrement

cor — *(Lat)* thorough(ly), with

cosmo — *(Gk)* universe

costo — *(Lat)* rib

cranio — *(Gk)* skull

cruci — *(Lat)* cross

cryo — *(Gk)* cold

crypto — *(Gk)* hidden

cteno — *(Gk)* rake, comb

cunei — *(Lat)* wedge

cupro — *(Lat)* bronze, copper

cymo — *(Gk)* wave

cysto — *(Gk)* bladder

cyto — *(Gk)* cell

dactylo — *(Gk)* finger

de — *(Lat)* down, not

deca — *(Gk)* ten

deci — *(Lat)* (a) tenth

demi — *(Lat)* half

demo — *(Gk)* common people

dendro — *(Gk)* tree

denti — *(Lat)* tooth

derm(at)o — *(Gk)* skin

deutero — *(Gk)* second

dia — *(Gk)* through

digit(i) — *(Lat)* finger

dino — *(Gk)* terrible

diplo — *(Gk)* double

di(s) — *(Gk/Lat)* apart

dodeca — *(Gk)* twelve

dorsi —, **dorso** — *(Lat)* back (of body)

dyna(mo) — *(Gk)* force, power

dys — *(Gk)* evil, bad, hard, difficult

e —, **ec** — *(Gk/Lat)* out

echino — *(Gk)* spiny

ecto — *(Gk)* outside, external

ef — *(Gk/Lat)* out)

el —, **em** —, **en** — *(Gk)* in(to)

encephalo — *(Gk)* brain

ennea — *(Gk)* nine

entero — *(Gk)* gut

ento — *(Gk)* inside, interior

eph — *(Gk)* on

epi — *(Gk)* on

entomo — *(Gk)* insect

eo — *(Gk)* dawn, early

equi — *(Lat)* equal

ergo — *(Gk)* work

erythro — *(Gk)* red

ethno — *(Gk)* race, nation

eu — *(Gk)* good

ex — *(Gk/Lat)* out

exo — *(Gk)* outside, external

extra — *(Lat)* outside, external

febri — *(Lat)* fever

ferri —, **ferro** — *(Lat)* iron

fissi — *(Lat)* split

fluvio — *(Lat)* river

galacto — *(Gk)* milk

gamo — *(Gk)* copulation, united

gastro — *(Gk)* stomach

gemmi — *(Lat)* bud

geo — *(Gk)* land, earth

geronto — *(Gk)* old age

glosso — *(Gk)* tongue

gluc —, **glyc** — *(Gk)* sweet

glyph —, **glypto** — *(Gk)* carving

gnatho — *(Gk)* jaw

gono — *(Gk)* reproduction (sexual)

grapho — *(Gk)* writing

gymno — *(Gk)* naked, nude

gyn(aec)o — *(Gk)* woman

haema(to) — *(Gk)* blood

hagio — *(Gk)* holy

halo — *(Gk)* salt, sea

haplo — *(Gk)* simple

hecto — *(Gk)* hundred

helico — *(Gk)* spiral

helio — *(Gk)* sun

hemi — *(Gk)* half

hepato — *(Gk)* liver

hepta — *(Gk)* seven

hetero — *(Gk)* different

hexa — *(Gk)* six

histo — *(Gk)* tissue

hodo — *(Gk)* path, way

holo — *(Gk)* complete, whole

homeo — *(Gk)* similar, like

homo — *(Gk)* same

hyalo — *(Gk)* glass

hydro — *(Gk)* water

hyeto — *(Gk)* rain

hygro — *(Gk)* wet

hylo — *(Gk)* matter

hymeno — *(Gk)* membrane

hyper — *(Gk)* above

hypno — *(Gk)* sleep

hypo — *(Gk)* under

hypso — *(Gk)* high

hystero — *(Gk)* womb

iatro — *(Gk)* medicine

ichthyo — *(Gk)* fish

igni — *(Lat)* fire

il —, im —, in — *(Lat)* against, in(to), not, on

inguino — *(Lat)* groin

inter — *(Lat)* between

intra —, intro — *(Lat)* inside, interior

ir — *(Lat)* against, in(to), not, on

iso — *(Gk)* equal

juxta — *(Lat)* close, near, beside

kerato — *(Gk)* horn

kinesi —, kineto — *(Gk)* movement

labio — *(Lat)* lip

lacto — *(Lat)* milk

lamelli — *(Lat)* plate, scale (of fish, etc)

lepido — *(Gk)* scale (of fish, etc)

lepto — *(Gk)* slender

leuko — *(Gk)* white

ligni — *(Lat)* wood

litho — *(Gk)* stone

logo — *(Gk)* word, speaking

luni — *(Lat)* moon

lyo —, lysi — *(Gk)* dissolving

macro — *(Gk)* large

magni — *(Lat)* great

mal(e) — *(Lat)* evil, bad

malaco — *(Gk)* soft

mega —, megalo — *(Gk)* great

melano — *(Gk)* black

mero — *(Gk)* part

meso — *(Gk)* middle

meta — *(Gk)* after, beyond, changed

metro — *(Gk)* measure

micro — *(Gk)* small

miso — *(Gk)* hatred

mono — *(Gk)* single, one

morpho — *(Gk)* shape

multi — *(Lat)* many

myelo — *(Gk)* spinal cord

mylo — *(Gk)* fungus

myo — *(Gk)* muscle

naso — *(Lat)* nose

nati — *(Lat)* birth

necro — *(Gk)* dead body

nec — *(Gk)* new

nepho — *(Gk)* cloud

nephro — *(Gk)* kidney

neuro — *(Gk)* nerve

nocti — *(Lat)* night

noso — *(Gk)* sickness

noto — *(Gk)* back (of body)

nycto — *(Gk)* night

ob —, oc — *(Lat)* against

octo —, octa — *(Gk/Lat)* eight

oculo — *(Lat)* eye

odonto — *(Gk)* tooth

of — *(Lat)* against

oleo — *(Lat)* oil

oligo — *(Gk)* few

ombro — *(Gk)* rain

omni — *(Lat)* all

oneiro — *(Gk)* dream

onto — *(Gk)* being, existence

oo — *(Gk)* egg

op — *(Lat)* against

ophio — *(Gk)* snake

opthalmo — *(Gk)* eye

ornitho — *(Gk)* bird

oro — *(Gk)* mountain

oro — *(Lat)* mouth

ortho — *(Gk)* straight

ossi — *(Lat)* bone

osteo — *(Gk)* bone

oto — *(Gk)* ear

ovi —, ovo — *(Lat)* egg

oxy — *(Gk)* sharp

pachy — *(Gk)* thick

palaeo — *(Gk)* ancient, old

pan(to) — *(Gk)* all

para — *(Gk)* close, near, beside

pari — *(Lat)* equal

patho — *(Gk)* suffering, disease

pedo — *(Gk)* child

penta — *(Gk)* five

per — *(Lat)* through, very

peri — *(Gk)* around, very

petro — *(Gk)* stone

phago — *(Gk)* eating

phanero — *(Gk)* visible

phlebo — *(Gk)* vein

phono — *(Gk)* sound

photo — *(Gk)* light

phreno — *(Gk)* brain

phyco — *(Gk)* seaweed

phyllo — *(Gk)* leaf

phylo — *(Gk)* species

physio — *(Gk)* nature

phyto — *(Gk)* plant

picro — *(Gk)* bitter

piezo — *(Gk)* pressure

pinni — *(Lat)* fin, web

pisci — *(Lat)* fish

plano — *(Lat),* flat (level)

pleuro — *(Gk)* side (of body)

plumbo — *(Lat)* lead (metal)

pluto — *(Gk)* riches

pluvio — *(Lat)* rain

pneumato — *(Gk)* breath, spirit

pneumo — *(Gk)* lung

polio — *(Gk)* grey matter

poly — *(Gk)* many

post — *(Lat)* after

pre — *(Lat)* before

preter — *(Lat)* beyond

primi — *(Lat)* first

pro — *(Gk)* before, forward

pro — *(Lat)* for, forward

proto — *(Gk)* first

pseudo — *(Gk)* false

psycho — *(Gk)* mind, soul, spirit

psychro — *(Gk)* cold

ptero — *(Gk)* wing

pulmo — *(Lat)* lung

pyo — *(Gk)* pus

pyro — *(Gk)* fire

quadri — *(Lat)* four

quinque — *(Lat)* five

re — *(Lat)* again

recti — *(Lat)* straight

reni — *(Lat)* kidney

retro — *(Lat)* backwards

rheo — *(Gk)* flow, current

rhino — *(Gk)* nose

rhizo — *(Gk)* root

saccharo — *(Gk)* sugar

sacro — *(Lat)* dedicated

sangui — *(Lat)* blood

sapro — *(Gk)* rot, decompose

sarco — *(Gk)* flesh

sauro — *(Gk)* lizard

scato — *(Gk)* excrement

scelero — *(Gk)* hard

schisto —, schizo — *(Gk)* split

se — *(Lat)* apart

sebi —; sebo — *(Lat)* fat(ty)

seleno — *(Gk)* moon

septi — *(Lat)* seven

sex — *(Lat)* six

sidero — *(Gkt)* iron

sidero — *(Lat)* star

somato — *(Gk)* body

somni — *(Lat)* sleep

speleo — *(Gk)* cave

spermato — *(Gk)* seed

spheno — *(Gk)* wedge

sphygmo — *(Gk)* pulse

spiro — *(Lat)* breath

splanchno — *(Gk)* guts

stato — *(Gk)* position

stauro — *(Gk)* cross

stelli — *(Lat)* star

steno — *(Gk)* short, narrow

sterco(ri) — *(Lat)* excrement

stereo — *(Gk)* solid

stomato — *(Gk)* mouth

stylo — *(Gk)* pillar

sub —, suc —, suf —, sum —, sup — *(Lat)* under

super —, supra — *(Lat)* above

sy(m) —, syl —, syn — *(Gk)* with

tachy — *(Gk)* rapid

tauto — *(Gk)* same

tele — *(Gk)* distant

teleo — *(Gk)* final

telo — *(Gk)* distant, final

terri — *(Lat)* land, earth

thalasso — *(Gk)* sea

thanato — *(Gk)* death

theo — *(Gk)* god

thermo — *(Gk)* heat

thio — *(Gk)* sulphur

toco — *(Gk)* birth, child

topo — *(Gk)* place

toxico — *(Gk)* poison

trachy — *(Gk)* rough

trans — *(Lat)* through, on the far side of

ultra — *(Lat)* beyond

uni — *(Lat)* single, one

vari(o) — *(Lat)* different

xeno — *(Gk)* foreign

zoo — *(Gk)* living

zygo — *(Gk)* double, yoke

Appendix 3:
Greek and Latin Suffixes

— **algia** *(Gk)* pain

— **androus** *(Gk)* man

— **archy** *(Gk)* rule, government

— **biosis** *(Gk)* life

— **blast** *(Gk)* bud

— **branch** *(Gk)* gills

— **carpous** *(Gk)* fruit

— **cele** *(Gk)* hollow

— **cephalic**, — **cephalous** *(Gk)* head

— **chrome** *(Gk)* colour

— **cidal**, — **cide** *(Lat)* kill

— **coccous** *(Gk)* berry-shaped

— **cracy, crat** *(Gk)* rule, government

— **dendron** *(Gk)* tree

— **derm** *(Gk)* skin

— **drome**, — **dromous** *(Gk)* run (race)

— **emia** *(Gk)* blood

— **fid** *(Lat)* split

— **fugal**, — **fuge** *(Lat)* run away from

— **gamy** *(Gk)* marriage

— **gen(ous)**, — **geny**, — **gony** *(Gk)* giving birth to, bearing

— **gnathous** *(Gk)* jaw

— **gnomy**, — **gnosis** *(Gk)* knowledge

— **gon** *(Gk)* angle

— **gonium** *(Gk)* seed

— **grade** *(Lat)* walking

— **gram**, — **graph(y)** *(Gk)* writing

— **hedral**, — **hedron** *(Gk)* side(d)

— **iasis** *(Gk)* disease

— **iatrics**, — **iatry** *(Gk)* medicine

— **itis** *(Gk)* inflammation

— **kinesis** *(Gk)* movement

— **lepsy** *(Gk)* fit, seizure

— **lith** *(Gk)* stone

— **logy** *(Gk)* science of, list

— **lysise**, — **lyte** *(Gk)* dissolving

— **machy** *(Gk)* battle, fight

— **mancy**, — **mantic** *(Gk)* foretelling

— **mania(c)** *(Gk)* craving

— **mere**, — **merous** *(Gk)* part

— **meter**, — **metry** *(Gk)* measure

— **morphic**, — **morphous** *(Gk)* shape

— **mycete** *(Gk)* fungus

— **nomy** *(Gk)* law of, science of

— **odont** *(Gk)* tooth

— **odynia** *(Gk)* pain

— **oid** *(Gk)* similar, like

— **oma** *(Gk)* tumour

— **opia** *(Gk)* eye, sight

— **opsia** *(Gk)* sight

— **opsis** *(Gk)* appearance

— **pathy** *(Gk)* suffering, disease

— **pennale** *(Lat)* wing

— **phage**, — **phagous**, — **phage** *(Gk)* eating

— **phany** *(Gk)* manifestation

— **phobe**, — **phobia** *(Gk)* fear

— **phone**, — **phony** *(Gk)* sound

— **phyllous** *(Gk)* leaf

— **phyte** *(Gk)* plant

— **plasia**, — **plasis** *(Gk)* growth

— **plasm** *(Gk)* matter

— **plast** *(Gk)* cell

— **plegia** *(Gk)* paralysis

— **plerous** *(Gk)* wing

— **rrhea**, — **rrhagia**, — **rrhagic** *(Gk)* flow

— **rrhaphy** *(Gk)* surgical stitching

— **saur** *(Gk)* lizard

— **scope**, — **scopy** *(Gk)* observe

— **sect(ion)** *(Gk)* cutting

— **soma**, — **some** *(Gk)* body

— **sophy** *(Gk)* wisdom

— **sperm(ous)** *(Gk)* seed

— **stichous** *(Gk)* row

— **stome**, — **stomous** *(Gk)* mouth

— **taxis**, — **taxy** *(Gk)* order

— **tomy** *(Gk)* cutting

— **trophy** *(Gk)* feed

— **tropous**, — **tropy** *(Gk)* turned

— **vorous** *(Lat)* eating